Propaganda has an ugly sound to many people in the United States. They think of it as being something the other side puts out, never their side. Yet propaganda as Gladys and Marcella Thum define it is as much a part of America as the flag or apple pie. It was propaganda that brought the thirteen colonies to the point of war with the British and that helped win the final victory. Propaganda has been a part of every war since. Propaganda has influenced almost every political campaign. Many such campaigns have been carefully planned to achieve maximum benefit from expensively prepared—and sometimes misleading—propaganda. Our newspapers and magazines are full of advertising propaganda. And even some of our laws and constitutional amendments have come about because of skillful propaganda campaigns.

Since the future is likely to bring even more propaganda than the past has seen, it is important to understand it, the authors say. To know the devices and to see how they have been and can be used, is to be better able to evaluate information and to come to one's own conclusions, not the conclusions someone else is advocating.

The Persuaders

Propaganda in War and Peace

Best wishes for the Missouri Center for the Book.

Gladys Thum

Marcella Thum

The Persuaders

Propaganda in War and Peace

Gladys & Marcella Thum

Illustrated with photographs

Atheneum   New York   1974

To Sylvia & Jules

Contents

The Persuaders

Propaganda in War and Peace

Introduction: May We Introduce–You, the Propagandist

SOME PEOPLE THINK propaganda is a new invention. It is not. From the time we lived in caves, we human beings have not only wanted to understand—and be understood—we have also wanted to persuade each other. We have always wanted something, and we have always tried to get it from the other fellow—sometimes with clubs, more often with words. That is why communication between people often includes propaganda devices. Many of these devices have not changed through the years because human emotions and reactions have not changed. The use of propaganda has increased in importance, however, because mass communication media—newspapers, radio, film and television— have greatly expanded. Instead of one person persuading

3

one other, one person now can persuade millions of people.

Some people say propaganda is "all lies" and is "bad" or only used by the "enemy" during wartime. Such people are themselves using the propaganda device of *Over-simplification.* Propaganda can be based on lies, or on half truths, or on truth. Propaganda devices can be employed for bad reasons—in selling a useless quack medicine—or for good reasons—in promoting a campaign against tuberculosis. And although propaganda has proven an effective weapon during wartime—always used by all sides—it is equally effective in peace.

American slaveholders used propaganda to promote slavery; American abolitionists used propaganda in their fight against slavery—and both sides believed they were in the right. For propaganda is based on use of human motivations, and human motivations may be illogical or logical, destructive or constructive, short-sighted or long-visioned, hating or loving. Adolf Hitler used propaganda; so did George Washington. So do we. So do you.

You don't recall using a propaganda device lately? See if any of the following sound like you—or like somebody you know.

COMMON PROPAGANDA DEVICES

THE APPEALS DEVICE. This device uses appeals to human emotions and desires in order to promote or "sell" *something else.* The *something else* is what is actually being offered. The following are only a few of the most frequently used appeals:

Sex Appeal—"If you buy this car, *all of the girls* will be running after you."

Snob-Status Appeal—"Susan, I know we can't afford it but *people in our position* have to belong to a country club."

Fear Appeal—"While you are out here fighting a war, *your girl back home is going around* with a draft dodger." Or: "Do you find other *people are avoiding you?* Use Zippo mouthwash."

Bandwagon or Join-the-Crowd Appeal—"Dad, *all of the other families on the block* have color TV."

Testimonial or Authority-Celebrity Appeal—"If the *top hitter in the National League* says that cereal is good, then it must be good."

Save-Money Appeal—"This [built-in-obsolescence] gadget is the *cheapest* on the market—*saves* you two dollars."

Plain-Folks Appeal—"Sure, he inherited ten billion dollars, is chairman of the board of General World Corporation, and candidate for President of the United States, but deep down he is just an *average citizen like* you—*plain, good folks,* washing dishes for his wife."

Youth Appeal—"Think *young*" (with a soda); "Look *young*" (with a soap).

David-and-Goliath Appeal—"You *big bully,* stop hitting that little guy"—just because he is shooting at you. Or: "We're *only number two*. We try harder."

Atrocity Appeal — *Their* soldiers slaughtered innocent children."

Humor Appeal—Any product presented as a bit funny. Thus, a foreign import car might advertise, "Think small!" Or a banana firm indicating its product is ripe might use, "We're yellow!"

The Appeals Device is probably the most common of all propaganda devices and the appeals used may overlap—thus, an advertisement of an automobile parked in front of a mansion with a beautiful girl at the wheel offers status and sex appeals combined. The car is what is being sold; the appeals are only a propaganda device.

THE DISTRACTION DEVICE. This device consists of pointing attention toward one thing in order to hide (or minimize) another. Thus, the politician: "Ah, what did you say, Mr. Jones? You didn't like my voting for the property tax. . . . Why, Mrs. Jones, what a beautiful baby you have there. Such a handsome little boy, Mr. Jones. What a lucky man you are. Looks just like you. . . ." Or: "Because of our new harvesting machines, fewer people on earth go hungry"— The Gigantic Harvester and Machine Gun Corporation.

LOGICAL-FALLACY DEVICE. This device uses what appears to be a logical, non-emotional approach, but the logic has flaws or gaps. In propaganda, two types of logical fallacies or flaws frequently appear:

The Hot-Potato Approach—This approach resembles the question, "Have you stopped beating your wife?" Whether the husband answers yes or no, he is in the wrong. In other words, this propaganda approach is phrased so that there can be no good reply. Communist propaganda against the United States in Africa might be phrased, "Have white Americans stopped killing black people?"

The 100-Percent Approach—This approach consists of putting all of the praise or blame on something that deserves only a part of the praise or blame. Thus, if one could estimate that about 80 percent of automobile accidents are caused by drivers, a propagandist for an automobile manufacturer, fighting against having to add costly new safety features to next year's model, might say, "Such safety features are useless. Everyone knows that drivers, not cars, cause the accidents."

MISLEADING ASSOCIATION DEVICE. This device connects or associates one thing with another. The two do have a remote connection or association, but not the one that is implied. This "misleading" implied association may appear as follows:

Political propaganda—"Presidential candidate Adlai Stevenson worked in the State Department at the same time as Alger Hiss, who has been convicted of conspiring for Communism."

Actual Association: Worked in same department.

Implied Association: Stevenson shared in Communist conspiracy.

War propaganda—"United States corporation profits doubled in 1968.—United States casualties doubled in Vietnam in 1968."

Actual Association: Both doubled in number.

Implied Association: Corporation profits were based on war casualties.

OVER-SIMPLIFICATION DEVICE. This device takes something that requires a long, balanced explanation and presents it too simply, leaving out necessary explanation. Usually, this device appears in the form of a slogan or a stereotype. Both forms appeal for emotional, not logical, support.

Slogans—A VOTE FOR JOHN DOE IS A VOTE FOR BALTIMORE.

CONSERVATIVE POLITICS WORK!

FORWARD WITH LABOR!

MAKE THE WORLD SAFE FOR DEMOCRACY!

FORD HAS A BETTER IDEA!

JOIN THE DODGE REBELLION!

Stereotype—This is a set form or picture that gives an individual the characteristics of his "type"—although he may have few or none of the characteristics. The stereotype over-simplifies the individual human being—and makes it difficult for others to see him as a human being and not just a "type." No human being is a "type." Here are a few of the

7

commonly used and accepted stereotypes of present and past. Perhaps you can think of some others.

Old Army sergeant
Old maid schoolteacher
Ozark hillbilly
Radical student demonstrator
"Typical" teen-ager.

SELECTION DEVICE. This device consists of exactly what its name says: a deliberate selection or choice in favor of whatever is being promoted. The device may appear in various forms; the following are a few of the more frequently used ones:

Selection: *"Out of Context"*—Words or sentences are taken out of a speech or a piece of writing. The part taken "out of context" distorts or twists what the complete speech or piece of writing said. Thus, if a book critic writes, "I find this new novel unbelievable. The author's ignorance of his subject is simply breathtaking," the advertisement for the book may quote the critic, but as follows: "Unbelievable. . . . simply breathtaking."

Selection: *The Scapegoat*—A single person or a group is selected or chosen as the scapegoat, to take the blame for whatever goes wrong. Hitler repeatedly used the Jewish people as the scapegoat for Germany's defeat in World War I; Communist China and The Soviet Union blame most of what goes wrong in the world on "imperialist" United States; "Communists" are frequently singled out as being to blame for social ills in the United States.

Selection: *Card Stacking (Including the Image)*—In Card Stacking, certain details are selected and then presented as if they represent the complete picture of a situation, an organization or a person. Corporations seek a good public "image"; so do political candidates. Naturally, the

8

characteristics presented, which can be true or false, are selected with an eye to public or voter reaction. Sometimes the over-simplified Stereotype, which comes ready-made— the "Lincoln type" or "White-hat cowboy hero type"— may be used in place of creating an individual "image."

Selection by False Emphasis—Someone or something is selected and then given too much or too little importance by receiving too much or too little newspaper space or radio-television time. In other words, if a hundred-dollar robbery is spread all over the front page and a million-dollar robbery is hidden in a one-paragraph story on the last page of a newspaper, which story will most people read? False emphasis can also include suppression of any information about any selected subject or person.

THE WORD DEVICES. These appear in three forms:

Name Calling—Precisely what the term indicates. This word device is always used *against* an individual, a cause or an idea. Name Calling can make us *form a judgment* without examining the complete evidence:

> POLICE THUGS CLUB DOWN COLLEGE STUDENTS (News headline)
>
> COMMUNIST HORDES BATTLE UNITED STATES TROOPS (News headline)
>
> "My political opponent is a *moss-backed reactionary.*"
> or:
> "My political opponent is a *Communist radical.*"

Loaded Words—The words are chosen for their good, neutral or bad flavor; in other words, they are chosen to create the effect the propagandist desires. In the following, your word choice depends on how you want the reader to feel about the Jones family:

> 1. John Jones is (economical) (thrifty) (stingy).
> 2. Mary Jones is (overweight) (stout) (fat).

9

3. Bill Jones is a(an) (enthusiast) (extremist) (fanatic).

Glittering Words—There are "Glittering Names" and "Glittering Generalities." Glittering Names are just the reverse of Name Calling. Instead of giving a person a bad name without evidence to support it, the propagandist gives a person a glittering good name, without evidence to support it:

>Benefactor of the People
>Standard-Bearer for the Right
>True Friend of the Poor Man

Glittering Generalities, like Glittering Names, mean different things to different people and are not defined as to what they mean at any given time in any given situation. All Glittering Names and Glittering Generalities "sound" good. The person using them in propaganda does not explain; he simply uses the words because they glitter. While Glittering Names refer to people, Glittering Generalities refer to ideas:

Freedom	Law and Order
Love	The American Way
Liberty	Patriotism

There is nothing wrong with these words, as long as the writer or speaker states clearly what *he* means by them and does not use them simply to give a good effect.

All of these popularly used propaganda devices cited may be employed separately or together. Slogans, for example, often use Glittering Words. It is worth noting too that in place of words, pictures and symbols can be used. A cartoonist using the symbol of the Nazi swastika is name calling someone a Nazi. A picture of a skull symbolizes the threat of death in any wartime propaganda appeals to bring about surrender. Flags can be used in place of the

Glittering Generality "patriotism" to cause a good effect—without further definition of what action lies behind the use of this patriotic symbol. And, of course, a picture of a beautiful girl or handsome man can be used in place of words to show sex appeal or romantic appeal.

PROPAGANDA STRATAGEMS

In addition to the popular devices, two stratagems are often used in lengthy propaganda campaigns:

REPETITION—If something is repeated often enough, many people come to accept it and to believe it, though they may not have done so at first. Repetition also causes people to remember.

CONFUSION—This strategy is not used often but can be important when employed nationally or internationally. The purpose of this long-term strategy is to stall or to confuse the opponent or opposition. The Soviet propagandists used the Confusion Stratagem for years, by swift changes of international attitudes from harsh accusations to sudden friendly overtures, followed by sudden blank silences and then sudden new demands. As a result, other nations had difficulty in deciding policies and responses.

We have said propaganda can support good or bad causes. Propaganda can also support neutral causes without moral purposes. Advertisers, like the rest of us, use propaganda devices. Their aim is to sell their products and stay in business. An advertiser may believe his product is good or even the best, but he also knows there are good products competing against his.

If asked, the advertiser might say that he is simply "educating" the public. Actually, he is propagandizing the public. Education teaches how to think; propaganda teaches what to think. If an advertiser wished to educate the public, he would have to give all the facts about his product and all the facts about his competitors products and then teach people how to evaluate all the facts given—an impossible task. If he wished only to make his product known to the public, he could simply name his product and its price. He does not normally do either, instead he tries to persuade the public to buy his product—and such persuasion involves propaganda devices.

What then is propaganda? There are many scholarly definitions, all somewhat similar, but, briefly:

> *Propaganda is deliberate promotion, usually emotional, by an individual or a group, using any form of communication, to create, change or control the attitudes and actions of others.*

This book, however, is not meant to be a study of propaganda devices, but rather to show how these devices have influenced the lives of people in the past and are influencing our lives today. For propaganda is a force out of the past, continuing in the present and giving evidence of becoming more important in the future. It is an influence that helps shape military, political, economic and social events yet it is seldom mentioned or is ignored completely in history books because it is so much a part of human communication that it does not seem an "event."

Propaganda, nonetheless, is a force that has changed history—and it is a force that can strike when least expected. For example, a winter's day in the year 1968 somewhere in the Sea of Japan . . .

Propaganda Events Today

JANUARY 23, 1968—The tiny U.S.S. *Pueblo,* a Navy ship, wallowed off the North Korean port of Wonsan. The *Pueblo* was doing a "watching" job for the United States. Soviet Russian trawlers were doing similar jobs for Communism off the coasts of free-world nations. Engaged in its routine intelligence patrol, the *Pueblo* stayed carefully outside the twelve-mile limit of Communist North Korea's territorial waters. The drab little ship blended with the sea swells.

Going about their routine jobs, the eighty-three crew members may have thought of themselves as communications specialists, technicians or able seamen, but certainly not what they and their ship were soon to become: instruments of a carefully planned world-wide propaganda campaign. On a ship armed only with .50 caliber machine guns, the U.S.S. *Pueblo* crewmen obviously were not expecting—or inviting—attack.

But attack came. Flags on a North Korean sub-chaser signaled, "Heave to or I will open fire." Three patrol boats joined the attack, and North Korean MIG fighter planes circled over the *Pueblo*. When the *Pueblo* tried to escape, point-blank North Korean fire wounded eleven U.S. crewmen, one fatally. Armed North Korean sailors overran the *Pueblo*'s decks. Within hours, the news shocked the world.

In the United States, some cried, "Declare war!" Others counseled patience. But one question that everyone asked was "Why did North Korea do it?" The naval vessel of one nation attacking the vessel of another on the open sea was an act of war. The *Pueblo*'s communication gear, although secret, was not valuable enough for North Korea to risk war for it. In any case, what did the North Korean Communist government expect to gain for such risk?

No one could answer that question completely. But one advantage that the North Koreans hoped to achieve became clear very shortly. Within a few days, North Korea released to world news media a propagandized confession of the *Pueblo*'s commander that his ship had entered North Korean territorial waters in a "sheer act of aggression." The United States was thus accused of deliberately inciting war—or at the very least of deliberately ignoring the rights of the small Asian nation.

The commander's torture-forced confession (the lives of his men were threatened) was only the beginning. The propaganda campaign that followed deliberately portrayed an "image" of the United States as a war-mongering bully whose bluff had been called. While the United States government negotiated to bring about the safe return of the crew, North Korean propagandists kept busy. Photographs of handwritten statements of *Pueblo* crewmen confessing their guilt as "war mongers" were sent to world news media. Films of Commander Bucher of the *Pueblo* appealing to the United States to apologize for its "aggression" appeared on world television. Radio Pyongyang, the official North Korean radio, broadcast claims that orders had been found aboard the *Pueblo* proving the ship was sent to operate within North Korean territorial waters. Films of the *Pueblo* crew in captivity, "imperialists" suitably humbled, were distributed.

Significantly, the voice of the *Pueblo*'s commander recorded on propaganda tapes was used to urge surrender over loudspeakers across the 151-mile demilitarized zone separating Communist North Korea from United States-allied South Korea. Although the anti-American propaganda had been sent world-wide, the North Korean regime apparently expected it to do the most damage among Asians—the people of South Vietnam, Thailand, Taiwan, the Philippines, Japan, and, most particularly, the people of South Korea. By humiliating the United States, making it "lose face," the North Koreans hoped to influence South Koreans and other Asians to have second thoughts about placing confidence in the protective might of the United States. In addition, of course, the prestige of North Korea and Communism was given a boost.

It was not until September, 1968, that United States officials began to believe that, as one official said, the North Koreans had "milked all possible propaganda value of the *Pueblo* affair and are now genuinely interested in winding it up."

But not quite yet—and not without some finishing touches. In December, 1968, Major General Woodward, chief of the United States negotiating team at Panmunjon, signed a humiliating document, written by the North Koreans, which, in effect, acknowledged the "guilt" of the United States in violating North Korean territorial waters and the "truth" of the crewmen's confessions. This propaganda document, Major General Woodward pointed out before signing, was contrary to facts, but he would sign because the United States wanted to free the *Pueblo* crewmen. The North Koreans publicized the acknowledgment of United States guilt—but not the general's disclaimer.

Thus far, the North Korean propagandists had succeeded in painting their image of the United States as a cowardly bully, and Asians and most of the rest of the world had viewed that image. Although the North Koreans had used primitive methods of torture to secure publicized confessions, they had used the most modern communications media—newspaper, radio, tapes, films, loudspeakers, television—to propagandize these "confessions." They had not waited for an event to happen that might be usable material. They had created an event and then an "image" and secured a world propaganda victory.

With the *Pueblo* crew of no further use to them, the North Koreans could expect added good publicity for their humanity in letting the United States "lackeys of the war mongers" go—and over the Christian Christmas Holidays, too. The timing of the release must have seemed excellent to the North Koreans.

It was not excellent. The timing was all wrong for North Korean propaganda, because another world-interest news event was slated to take place during these same Christmas holidays. Although the *Pueblo* crew was released with appropriate North Korean propaganda and fanfare, the world's eyes and ears were focused elsewhere—on the moon.

The release of the *Pueblo* crew was, temporarily at least,

The U.S.S. *Pueblo* shown underway off the coast of San Diego, California.
U.S. Navy

DATE: December 23, 1968, Panmunjom, Korea. Crew of the U.S.S. *Pueblo*
crossing the bridge to freedom following their release by North Korea.
U.S. Navy

DATE: December 23, 1968. On the same date the *Pueblo* prisoners were being released with appropriate propaganda statements from the North Koreans as to America's "confession of guilt," the Apollo 8 spacecraft had been launched and was heading for the moon. Live television photographs like this one, showing asstronaut Borman at the controls of the spacecraft, turned the attention—and the headlines—of the world away from the *Pueblo* prisoners. *National Aeronautics and Space Administration*

For the first time in human history, mankind penetrated the mysterious "far side" of the moon and were able to photograph the first "earth rise," 240,000 statute miles from the spacecraft. Suddenly men on earth were seeing their planet from another body in space. Feats like the Apollo space flights, though not propagandic in origin, can add immeasurably to the "good" image of a nation. *National Aeronautics and Space Administration*

The returning Apollo 8 astronauts, Borman, Lovell and Anders, wave at cheering crewmen of the U.S.S. *Yorktown,* their recovery ship. The three astronauts were the first men ever to orbit the moon and to see its mysterious far side. Their trip, covered by live television from their spacecraft, told the world that men could indeed reach the moon. In the eyes of the world, the "bad" image that North Korean propagandists had built out of the *Pueblo* incident was diminished by the heroic image of American spacemen. *National Aeronautics and Space Administration*

A leader of Students for a Democratic Society begins working up student protest at Columbia University, New York, almost as soon as a new semester begins. The protests led later to an angry student–police confrontation in spring, 1968. *Fred W. McDarrah*

only a minor piece of world news, sandwiched in between fascinating, suspenseful accounts of three men traveling across seemingly endless miles of space and orbiting the moon. With the astounding success of the United States' Apollo 8 moonshot and the television coverage from the space ship, people all over the world became aware that within their lifetimes (actually within a year), men were going to land on the moon. With Apollo 8's clear pictures, the people of the world even saw for themselves how their earth looked from the moon.

The well-trained North Korean propagandists had been tripped up by space technology—and by an equally modern development of propaganda. Instantaneous world-wide communication now makes the timing of a propaganda event almost as important as the event itself. Some propagandists said the American government had purposely timed the signing of the humiliating document that released the *Pueblo* crew so that the release coincided with the moonshot. Few can say if the timing was a consideration. In any case, the effect was the same. The timing of the *Pueblo* crew release was a propaganda score for the United States.

It can readily be seen why. The successful moonshot made the United States a hero in the eyes of the world. The "image" of a nation, like that of a person, cannot portray a hero and a villain at the same time. The bad "image" of the United States given by the *Pueblo* propaganda was temporarily obscured.

Yet because the North Korean regime had used a created event for propaganda with some world effect, they had reason to try it again. In April, 1969, a pair of North Korean MIG fighter planes shot down well away from North Korean air space this time, an American Navy EC121, a lumbering communications-intelligence airplane that American reporters promptly labled the "Flying Pueblo." Thus, the grim intelligence and propaganda game continues in international affairs today. But though it seems so modern, such use of propaganda is not new. The almost legendary Chinese Sun Tzu wrote instructions on the use of propaganda in his Book of War in the fifth century, B.C. He included instructions for dropping propaganda leaflets from kites to incite the enemy to surrender. He also wrote on the use of noise to paralyze and fool enemy soldiers. It is recorded that about 202 B.C., a general fighting a new Han dynasty emperor managed to escape annihilation by flying kites with strings that made noises on a breezy dark night, making the emperor's soldiers believe guardian spirits spoke to them, causing them to flee the scene. And in 1232 A.D. in China, it is recorded Chinese forces dropped propaganda messages from kites, trying to incite prisoners of the Mongols to revolt against their captors.

To aid in his sweep across Europe, Genghis Khan piled up human skulls after destroying a town, using Fear-Appeal propaganda to make neighboring towns lose the will to fight. Queen Elizabeth I of England spread atrocity stories of the horrors of the Spanish Inquisition to arouse the English people against the Spanish Armada. And Phillip II of Spain circulated atrocity stories about Elizabeth's treatment of Catholics to gain English Catholic support against the Protestant Elizabeth.

Propaganda in war or peace can be found throughout human history whenever men by deliberately chosen methods have tried to influence each other's actions. Yet the word "propaganda" is less than four centuries old. The term came into use through the Roman Catholic Church. To combat the ideas of Protestants like Luther and Calvin, Pope Gregory XV in 1622 created the Sacra Congregation for the Propagation of the Faith. The purpose of this congregation (or group) was to propagandize—that is, by specific methods to deliberately spread the beliefs of the Roman Catholic faith throughout the world. The word "propaganda" then did not have the bad connotation it so often has today.

We all use propaganda, though we seldom admit it. More specifically, we use the common propaganda devices, and they are used on us. Propaganda can be seen and heard everywhere: in our homes, in the market place, in politics, and even in education—in and out of class.

We can point, for example, to a college campus where students are milling about with picket signs, protesting current events. The protests may or may not be "good," depending on our viewpoints. In considering propaganda, however, viewpoints do not matter. What does matter is that all of the protest signs are using propaganda devices. One sign uses Misleading Association: "OUR COLLEGE BOARD CHAIRMAN WENT TO SCHOOL WITH RACIST GEORGE WALLACE." Another sign employs an Over-simplification slogan: "STUDENTS ARE THE COLLEGE: STUDENTS SHOULD RUN THE COLLEGE." Another sign, protesting dormitory-hour restrictions, utilizes Glittering Words: "LOVE IS FREE. STUDENTS SHOULD BE FREE TO LOVE."

An apparently angry young student shouts to the crowd. He uses Name Calling: "Kidnap the dean, the Establishment pig!"

A few students cheer. Others shake their heads, frowning. Still others—most of the crowd—hesitate—look at the ground.

The intense student speaker tries again, crying out the Bandwagon Appeal: "We're all in this together. Burn down the administration building and run the dean out. We've got to stand together!"

He is still screaming at the crowd of students when the

police arrive. He leads some of the students in a rush on the police. As he is finally dragged off with other struggling protestors, he cries to a nearby friend triumphantly: "We did it! They clubbed Jim! The photographer was right there. Police brutality! No freedom of speech. Lots of guys will join us now!"

And the young speaker—for good cause or bad—is hauled off to jail, having manufactured an inflammatory news event, deliberately created in the same manner as the North Koreans "manufactured" the much-propagandized *Pueblo* event.

Thus the force of propaganda molds events today, as it shaped those of yesterday. Since propaganda devices are firmly based on natural human responses, the devices remain essentially the same; only the events change.

In our own American history, the force of propaganda has played an important, if often unacknowledged, role. The propaganda has gone unacknowledged in most cases because many Americans have an idea that propaganda is something distasteful, something underhanded that other countries and other peoples may use, but not us.

Ironically, one of the master propagandists of all time was an American patriot—Samuel Adams. It was his skillful and effective use of propaganda that united the American people behind a common cause and, later, was instrumental in helping to win a war against overwhelming odds.

His cause was freedom—and the war was the American Revolution.

War Propaganda and the American Revolution: The Pen and the Sword

Practically every American has heard of the Boston Massacre. If asked what happened that March night in 1770, most Americans would say, "A troop of British soldiers shot down in cold blood a group of unarmed American patriots." Is that what happened? Not exactly.

That night in Boston a lone British sentry was on duty at the Customs House on King Street. Small boys began pelting him with snowballs, taunting him, calling him "Lobsterback." The people of Boston resented the British soldiers, quartered in their city to quell colonial protests against royal taxes. Rowdies and ne'er-do-wells from the nearby wharf area quickly joined the boys, along with curious passersby, until a crowd of about sixty had gathered. The sentry, alarmed, called out the guard.

Ten British soldiers, armed with muskets, ran to the sentry's aid and ordered the crowd to disperse. The boys ran off. But many of the men stayed, most of them still roisterous, eager for a fight. They picked up clubs, stones, bottles, and threw them at the soldiers. Several soldiers were hit. One was knocked down. Outnumbered, provoked and afraid, the soldiers lowered their muskets into firing position. A British captain, Thomas Preston, appeared on the scene and cried, "Don't fire! Don't fire!"

His cry came too late. A volley rang out in the cold night air. Men crumpled to the ground, their blood staining the white snow a bright crimson. Both soldiers and colonists stared down in dismay at the fallen men. The officer ordered retreat.

Shortly thereafter, the British soldiers involved were tried. Two of the soldiers were convicted by the Boston jury, not of murder but of manslaughter, and were branded on the hand and dismissed. The remainder of the soldiers and Captain Preston were acquitted. The jury? Not British officers but Boston citizens. The soldiers' attorney? John Adams, later to become second President of the United States.

Then why has this incident, which was quite simply a group of battered and outnumbered soldiers firing into a mob that was attacking them, come down in our history books as "the Boston Massacre"? The answer can be summed up in the name of one man: Samuel Adams. Samuel Adams, considered a failure and a black sheep by his family, called a "radical" and "agitator" by his contemporaries, was a man who despised tyranny and was dedicated to liberty. He believed the colonies could obtain their freedom and throw off the yoke of British rule only by arousing the emotions of the colonists, binding them together against a common enemy, the British.

The King Street tragedy he turned into an "atrocity" story, deliberately inflaming public opinion and stirring up hatred against the British government. Some historians have even speculated that Adams himself deliberately helped gather the crowd that eventually provoked the shooting. In either case, Samuel Adams set about propagandizing. He spoke at town meetings, taverns, hostels, wherever he could, denouncing the King Street soldiers (and thereby through Misleading Association, all British soldiers) as cold-blooded murderers and depicting the American victims as innocent, patriotic martyrs. He had broadsides and leaflets distributed throughout the American colonies, with accusations containing emotionally Loaded Words like "massacre" to show the Americans' innocence and "murder" to show the British guilt, and added such phrases as "wallowing in their gore" to show British callousness.

To these carefully selected words of Samuel Adams, calculated to arouse the anti-British anger of American readers, were added pamphlets and leaflets written by other equally ardent believers in freedom. Among those who followed Adams' lead was his friend, Paul Revere, who struck off and distributed an engraving of the "massacre." This famous engraving supposedly pictured the event as it happened but, if you look closely, you will see it is actually pictorial propaganda. Soon, Samuel Adams' distorted version of the tragedy became widely accepted as the truth throughout the colonies.

Although the Massachusetts Historical Society, more than a century later in 1887, aware of the truth, protested the raising of a monument to the victims of "the Boston Massacre," most Americans, because of Samuel Adams, still think of the King Street incident as a cold-blooded massacre and the Americans involved as innocent martyrs, enshrined among our first national heroes. For Samuel

Adams, however, the propagandistic use of the Boston shooting was only the beginning of a long campaign to inflame the colonists to revolt against the British.

It was a revolt that did not come overnight. Adams' anti-British propaganda and agitation took several years to achieve its end. For the colonists were accustomed to British rule and considered themselves British subjects. And the colonies were thinly settled with people, too spread out to feel involved with each other. Also, revolution was a serious and dangerous step and, against a powerful country like England, must have seemed to many a hopeless cause. In addition, the colonists for the most part were content with things as they were. They were not so personally engaged with the British government in their daily lives as to feel concerned. In short, they were a "silent majority" who were not ready to do anything radical.

In order to shake the apathy and indifference of the people, Adams used an ancient propaganda device: Appeal to Fear. To do this, he helped to form and then received the aid of the Sons of Liberty, a group of men dedicated to agitating against the British—and against any colonists who sympathized with British rule. American colonists who showed loyalty to the king by buying imported British goods were denounced publicly through broadsheets distributed by the Sons of Liberty. The names of loyalist merchants were circulated on a blacklist and their shops boycotted.

But the Sons of Liberty did not rely alone on verbal Appeals to Fear, through threats and economic coercion. The Tory publisher John Mein was hanged in effigy and physically attacked, as were other loyalist printers. James Rivington in New York was burned in effigy and his printing press destroyed by the Sons of Liberty. Samuel Adams put to work early an important rule of propaganda: silence or eliminate opposition newspapers so that only stories and propaganda favorable to your cause will be read or reach the ears of the people.

Adams' master propaganda stroke, however, was an idea he proposed on November 2, 1772, at a Boston town meeting. It was a simple plan, but a shrewd and necessary one. Arousing temporary hatred of British tyranny was not enough. If rebellion were to come and to succeed, all of the people in all of the colonies from Massachusetts to Georgia had to be united. And to be united each colony must be kept informed of what the other colonies were doing and saying. So at Adams' suggestion the Committees of Correspondence were formed.

These committees, established in every important town, linked their members through a continual exchange of letters. A web of correspondence was formed that tied all the thirteen colonies together. These letters unified and informed people. But they did more. The letters—regularly printed by colonial newspapers—made certain that anti-British charges reached all points of the colonies, influencing public opinion, shaping attitudes and arousing resistance against the crown. The Committees of Correspondence became in effect a propagandist arm of a national government —before there even was a national government.

When the Revolutionary War began, Adams was joined by another outstanding American propagandist and dedicated lover of freedom: Thomas Paine. Paine used emotion-stirring words, dramatic, yet simple language filled with ringing phrases that were easily remembered, as well as Name Calling and ridicule of King George in order to downgrade the monarch in the minds of the colonists. Although other men, such as James Otis and John Dickinson, also wrote pamphlets urging liberty, their writings were more sober, and were directed toward the educated men of

The following text appears within the engraving:

Unhappy Boston! see thy Sons deplore,
Thy hallow'd Walks besmear'd with guiltless Gore,
While faithless P—n and his savage Bands,
With murd'rous Rancour stretch their bloody Hands;
Like fierce Barbarians grinning o'er their Prey,
Approve the Carnage, and enjoy the Day.

If scalding drops from Rage from Anguish Wrung
If speechless Sorrows lab'ring for a Tongue,
Or if a weeping World can ought appease
The plaintive Ghosts of Victims such as these;
The Patriot's copious Tears for each are shed,
A glorious Tribute which embalms the Dead.

But know Fate summons to that awful Goal,
Where Justice strips the Murd'rer of his Soul:
Should venal C—ts the scandal of the Land,
Snatch the relentless Villain from her Hand,
Keen Execrations on this Plate inscrib'd,
Shall reach a Judge who never can be brib'd.

The unhappy Sufferers were Messᵣˢ Samᴸ Gray, Samᴸ Maverick, Jamˢ Caldwell, Crispus Attucks & Patᴸ Carr
Killed. Six wounded; two of them (Christᵣ Monk & John Clark) Mortally

---

THE BOSTON MASSACRE (1770), Paul Revere—American, 1735–1818. In his engraving of the Boston "Massacre," Paul Revere placed a sign that said "Butcher's Hall" over the British Custom House and depicted British Captain Preston as deliberately ordering a volley against a group of harmless, helpless Bostonians. The engraving used such Loaded Words as "Bloody Massacre," and the British troops were Name-called "savage bands" and "fierce barbarians." When the soldiers were brought to trial, jurors were warned against "prints that add wings to fancy." *National Gallery of Art, Washington, D.C., Rosenwald Collection*

Samuel Adams—American colonial patriot who fiercely sought independence from Great Britain with the weapon of words. *Library of Congress*

Revolutionary War blacklist distributed by Sons of Liberty. Fear Appeals of such public denunciation and economic boycott served to make many wavering colonists support the patriot cause. *Massachusetts Historical Society*

WILLIAM JACKSON,

an *IMPORTER*; at the

BRAZEN HEAD,

North Side of the TOWN-HOUSE,

and *Oppofite the Town-Pump, in*

Corn-hill, B O S T O N.

It is defired that the Sons and Daughters of *LIBERTY,* would not buy any one thing of him, for in fo doing they will bring Difgrace upon *themfelves,* and their *Pofterity,* for *ever* and *ever,* AMEN

London cartoon of Bostonians "Paying the Excise Man," or tarring and feathering. The cartoon was based on what happened to John Malcomb, a Tory exciseman who tried to collect the tea tax in Boston in 1774. Even before Revolutionary War fighting began, the patriot "Sons of Liberty" were using Fear Appeals to overcome opposition. *Library of Congress*

This famous cartoon by Benjamin Franklin first appeared in the *Pennsylvania Gazette* on May 9, 1754. It was reprinted all over the American colonies in the years before the Revolutionary War. Its Appeal was simple: The colonies must unite in order to survive. *New York Public Library*

Picture of one of Washington's backwoods soldiers, with his famous fringed hunting shirt and long rifle. Washington ordered more soldiers put into this "uniform" early in the war. The British soldiers feared the sharpshooting ability of the frontiersman and his rifle, nicknamed the "Widow and orphan maker." *Keith Wilbur,* Picture Book of the Continental Soldier (*Stackpole*)

This contemporary picture of the Battle of Bunker Hill, 1775, was drawn by Johann Ramberg, a German. It appeared in *Allegemeinisches Historisches Taschenbuch*, published 1784 in Berlin. *The Metropolitan Museum of Art, Bequest of Charles Allen Munn, 1924*

PROSPECT HILL.	BUNKER's HILL.
I. Seven Dollars a Month. —	I. Three Pence a Day.
II. Frefh Provifions, and in Plenty. —	II. Rotten Salt Pork.
III. Health. — — — — —	III. The Scurvy.
IV. Freedom, Eafe, Affluence and a good Farm.	IV. Slavery, Beggary and Want.

The Bunker Hill leaflet—American propaganda tossed at British soldiers. The same Appeals—food, money, medical care—are used in psychological warfare leaflets today. *Paul M. A. Linebarger*

Benjamin Franklin (standing center in dark suit) went to France in 1776 to negotiate a treaty for the American colonies. Known as a scientist in Europe, he was immediately popular with the French court. Despite his age (70 years), he wielded influence with the ladies as well as the gentlemen there. A newspaperman by profession, he was aware of the persuasive powers of propaganda. His efforts helped to bring French military support and European sympathy for the independence of the colonies. *Library of Congress*

33

property. Paine appealed directly to the common man. His famous pamphlet *Common Sense* is credited with doing more to inflame the emotions of the colonists against the British monarchy than any other document.

A century and a half later, the man in charge of American propaganda activities in World War I, George Creel, referred to Thomas Paine as "a master propagandist who played upon the hearts of the Colonists with a strong, sure touch. It is not too much to say that his pen was no less mighty than the sword of Washington."

George Washington must have thought so, too. During the bitter war year of 1776, Washington ordered read aloud in every one of his camps, words from another of Paine's pamphlets, entitled *The Crisis:*

"These are the times that try men's souls. The summer soldier and the sunshine patriot will, in this crisis, shrink from the service of their country; but he that stands it now, deserves the love and thanks of man and woman. Tyranny, like hell, is not easily conquered . . ."

George Washington himself did not depend entirely on the sword. He recognized the power of words to arouse the soldiers' will to stand and fight—or retreat and run. Not only did he support the publication of colonial patriot newspapers to help unite the colonists behind him, but he also encouraged the dissemination of rumors that spread fear and dissent among the enemy. And he became a propagandist himself.

One of his propaganda efforts began when more than a thousand volunteer backwoodsmen, rugged men in buckskins, joined his army. Undisciplined, these frontiersmen made poor soldiers. In fact, Washington had to courtmartial an entire platoon for "disobedient and mutinous behavior." But the frontiersmen had one great virtue: they could shoot much farther and more accurately with their long rifles than other soldiers could with their muskets. Washington encouraged stories of the deadly accuracy of the frontiersmen to be placed in colonial newspapers. One such story in the *Pennsylvania Press* carried a Fear-Appeal warning to the British: "The worst of them [frontiersmen] will put a ball into a man's head at a distance of 150 or 200 yards, therefore advise your officers who shall hereafter come out to America to settle their affairs in England before their departure." It was reported, perhaps too optimistically, that when stories reached England of these "shirt-tail men, with their cursed twisted gun" recruitment in the British army dropped abruptly.

When the time was ripe, Washington gave a further twist to his propaganda. Taking advantage of the fears of the British soldiers (some of whom were already acquainted with the deadly aim of American frontiersmen from the French-Indian wars), Washington suggested that a number of his American troops who were *not* backwoodsmen should adopt the frontiersmen's distinctive fringed leather hunting shirt and long rifles, because such a uniform "carried no small terror to the enemy who thinks every such person a complete marksman." The rifles these men carried were, of course, simply weapons for military battle. They became weapons for propaganda as well when American propagandists publicized them, exaggerating their prowess, to instill fear in the enemy soldiers *before* battle.

Even more effective than this weapon propaganda, were the new efforts of the untiring Committees of Correspondence. At the instigation of Samuel Adams, they had helped to unite public opinion in the colonies against the British. Now the committees dealt with another propaganda need: to destroy the morale of the enemy soldier.

At the Battle of Bunker Hill, the American forces, poorly trained and low on ammunition, held Prospect Hill; the

35

British forces, facing them, held Bunker Hill. The American soldiers were furnished with propaganda leaflets, which they were told to wrap around bullets or rocks to make them "fly well" and heave them into British entrenchments. Although the delivery method left something to be desired, the propagandist appeals were clearly stated: better pay, better food, better health, better treatment if the British soldiers shifted to the other—the American—side. What was not stated was what the leaflet was actually "selling"—desertion and the risk of death in front of a firing squad if caught.

Although the effect of the Bunker Hill propaganda leaflets was not recorded, the American colonial propagandists are known to have been highly successful in a later attempt. This time the Committees of Correspondence aimed their propaganda at the under-paid, poorly fed, badly treated Hessian soldiers that had been hired by the British army. The colonial assembly passed a law granting a German captain who deserted and brought with him forty men: "800 acres, four oxen, one bull, three cows and four hogs." Under the law, even a German private who deserted was offered 50 acres and livestock. The law was translated into German, by the Committees of Correspondence, printed, and distributed to Hessian troops. What this propaganda appeal actually was "selling" was desertion. It sold well. Statistics show that after the war, of the 30,000 Germans hired to fight, only slightly more than half returned to Germany. A few had died from wounds and disease, but thousands more had deserted; many had joined the American army and fought against their former comrades.

Stung by the success of the American propaganda leaflets, the British tried propaganda, too. In 1779, the British General Clinton issued a proclamation promising freedom and security to any Negro slave who came over to the British. Many did. South Carolina lost 25,000 slaves, and Georgia and Virginia many thousands more. The slaves who responded to the propaganda assumed they would receive the appeal—freedom—when they took the article being sold—desertion of their masters. Unfortunately, propaganda appeals need not be "real." After the war, many of these black people who had believed the propaganda were resold in the West Indies or forced to turn fugitive. Although some were trained by the British and put into military units, only a few hundred managed to leave the country with the British troops.

In view of the lack of faith behind this appeal, it is satisfactory to record that this particular propaganda backfired on the British. They thought that mass desertion of slaves would bring the colonial South to its knees, fearful of slave uprisings, ready to admit defeat. Instead, many powerful Southern slave owners, who otherwise might have remained loyal to the British, were outraged by Clinton's proclamation and became firm revolutionists.

The revolutionary propagandists had attempted to accomplish what was to become standard procedure for later, more modern psychological warfare campaigns:

1. Unite the people against a common foe.
2. Destroy the morale of enemy troops.

A third and equally essential task remained: Influence any and all foreign allies to your cause. If such countries as France, Spain or Holland could be persuaded to help, it would mean survival to the new republic. But established royal governments seldom wished to ally themselves with new revolutionary republics. Revolutionaries in the eighteenth century were regarded with even more suspicion and distrust than they are today. However, American propaganda efforts overseas were assisted by two factors.

First: France, Spain and Holland feared and were jealous

of England's power. Second: the Continental Congress, with uncommonly good sense, sent Benjamin Franklin to serve as commissioner from America to France. Already admired in French scientific circles and surprisingly effective in winning the affection of the French people, Franklin, the diplomat, was well aware of what his job was. He had to publicize America's side of the war, erase suspicion of American revolutionaries and increase the European feeling of dislike toward England.

Franklin had had experience in the work. He had been in England at the time of the battle of Lexington. An American Salem clipper ship had managed to beat by eleven days the crossing of a British sloop bringing the news of the battle to England. Promptly, Franklin had spread the American version of the battle to English and European newspapers—naturally, with blame for the battle placed squarely on the British. When the British sloop and the British report had appeared with accusations of "treasonous minutemen" at Lexington, the British story had been anti-climatic and had already been discounted.

With this experience behind him, Franklin, arriving as American commissioner in France, immediately began placing pro-American stories in as many French newspapers as possible. And though England was also flooding Europe with news stories giving the British version of what was happening in the colonies, Franklin also managed, through friends, to place favorable American accounts of the war in Dutch, German and Irish newspapers.

So important did Franklin consider the steady flow of pro-American news and propaganda into European publications that he suggested to the Continental Congress that they use special light, fast sailing ships to send him regular news. With this news he could "refute the false news of our adversaries."

The Continental Congress, however, could not afford to supply fast news ships for Franklin. And, although the Committees of Correspondence tried to send American newspapers and letters to France, the British navy captured often the ships that carried them. So, unable to count on a regular supply of information from home, Franklin improvised.

As aware as Samuel Adams of the propaganda value of an atrocity story, Franklin arranged to have printed in European newspapers a letter supposedly sent by the Seneca Indians (allies of the English) to the British governor in Canada. In the letter the Senecas bragged about sending eight packages of American scalps—including those of women and children—to King George to show Indian "faithfulness."

The letter was what is often called "black propaganda"—propaganda that does not reveal its true source. Some historians believe Franklin wrote the letter. No one knows. As propaganda, it was brilliant. French and Dutch, even English, citizens read the letter and reacted with horror and revulsion toward the British for employing savages to fight their war. Franklin also publicized in Dutch newspapers stories of cruel treatment of American prisoners of war by the British. These stories, many of which were based on truth, also helped rouse sympathy for the American cause.

While Franklin was spreading his propaganda abroad, in the colonies another "atrocity" rumor began: that the British had deliberately caused a smallpox epidemic in Boston by sending newly inoculated soldiers among the people—just before the evacuation of British troops from the city. Many citizens of Boston believed this "atrocity" rumor. General Washington even warned his troops not to enter the city without permission "as the enemy with a malicious assiduity, have spread the infection of smallpox through all parts of the town." The rumor was spread by American sympathizers in Europe. It can be considered the first appearance in history of germ warfare propaganda, used later by Communists against Americans in the modern-day war in Korea.

Partly as a result of these efforts, by the end of the war, France, Holland and Spain were supporting the American cause. France, of course, actually sent vitally needed troops, troops that helped to bring about the British surrender at Yorktown.

Compared to the elaborate and costly propaganda campaigns conducted by modern governments in wartime, the American revolutionists' efforts must be regarded as primitive. Yet, the techniques used by Samuel Adams, Thomas Paine and Benjamin Franklin have been studied and copied by many past and present-day governments.

In fact, less than a hundred years later, in a war with the United States, a Mexican leader took a leaf from our American propaganda history. He turned this propaganda, ironically enough, upon United States troops.

War Propaganda of the Nineteenth and Early Twentieth Centuries: The Beginnings of War

IT WAS SEPTEMBER 13, 1847, during the last days of the war between Mexico and the United States. Outside of Mexico City, but within sight of the Castle of Chapultapec, thirty men with nooses around their necks were lined up on carts beneath a long gallows. As the American flag was raised in victory over Chapultapec, an American officer gave a signal—and the carts were driven out from under the men, all American soldiers.

What crime had these men committed to be hanged by their own people? They were some of the 250 American soldiers who had responded to the following propaganda leaflet distributed behind American lines by Mexican General Mariano Arista:

Soldiers:

I warn you in the name of justice, honor, and your own interest and self respect to abandon this desperate and unholy cause and become peaceful citizens of our country. I guarantee you a half section of land, or 320 acres, to settle on free. Lands shall be given to officer, sergeant and corporal according to rank, privates receiving 320 acres as stated.

The soldiers who had responded and deserted were mostly recent immigrants to the United States. They had learned to resent the harsh U.S. military discipline of the day and, hungering for land, had joined the Mexican army, forming the San Patricio battalion. Aware that if they were captured they would be hanged, they fought against their former American comrades so fiercely that the Mexican General Santa Anna had other such broadsheets printed, hoping to entice more American soldiers to the Mexican side.

The Appeals—land and honor—were the same as those used by American propagandists against Hessian soldiers in the Revolutionary War. These attractive appeals, offered once again, were attached to what was really being sold: desertion and possible death. All of the soldiers who formed the San Patricio Battalion were killed or captured during the fighting at Churubusco in 1847. Fifty in all were hanged because they responded to the propaganda leaflets.

Leaflets were used even more widely in the American Civil War of 1861–65—and a few of them were delivered by drops from unmanned balloons. However they were distributed, some people of the day felt their use was improper. Lieutenant General Longstreet of the Confederate army wrote in January, 1864, to Major General Foster of

42

the Union army: "The immediate object of this circulation among our soldiers seems to be to induce them to quit our ranks. . . . I respectfully suggest, for your consideration, the propriety of communicating any view that your government may have upon this subject through me, rather than by handbills circulated among our soldiers. The few men who may desert under promise held out . . . cannot be men of character or standing."

Union Major General Foster replied, "You are correct in the supposition that the great object in view in the circulation . . . is to induce those now in rebellion against the government to lay aside their arms. . . . The immediate effect is to cause many men to leave your ranks to return home, or come within our lines . . . it has been thought proper to issue an order announcing the favorable terms on which deserters will be received. However . . . I embrace with pleasure the opportunity thus afforded to enclose twenty copies each of these documents and rely upon your generosity and desire for peace to give publicity to the same among your officers and men. . . ."

Whether this tongue-in-cheek offer to General Longstreet was accepted, we do not know.

Newspapers with Southern sympathies also helped build up Confederate resistance against the North, using Fear and Hatred Appeals and Name Calling. The Richmond, Virginia, *Examiner* described Union soldiers as "brutal" men "drunken with wine, blood and fury" who "plunder the property, ravish the women, burn the house and proceed to the next." Union newspapers used the same devices. Both Northern and Southern newspapers accused the other side of atrocities to prisoners. Both sides used False Emphasis, playing down defeats and playing up victories in small skirmishes as triumphs in great battles. And like George Washington, Confederate General Robert E. Lee used newspaper propaganda effectively. Helped by the *Whig* and the *Enquirer,* both Richmond, Virginia, newspapers, he managed to fool Northern General McClellan, in nearby Washington, D.C., with false reports of troop movements.

But, although newspapers on both sides in the Civil War contained much war propaganda, it was not until the time of the Spanish-American War that newspapers again became the tremendously important propaganda tool they had been during the Revolutionary War. In fact, newspaper propaganda is historically credited with virtually creating the Spanish-American War!

The war was even called, by some historians, "Hearst's War," because of the role played in it by William Randolph Hearst, publisher of the *New York Journal.* The year was 1896, a time of cutthroat competition between newspapers for circulation—there were no radios, films or television to influence the public. It was also the year when revolutionaries were stirring in Spanish possessions such as Cuba, seeking to gain independence. Partly to incite sympathy for the Cuban rebels and partly to increase circulation, Hearst set about deliberately inflaming American public opinion against Spain. Again and again he used such common propaganda devices in his newspaper as:

Name Calling: The Spanish Governor of Cuba, Captain-General Valeriano Weyler, was referred to as "Butcher Weyler."

Atrocity story: Lurid, so-called eyewitness reports were published of the torturing by the Spanish of Cuban women and children, of Spanish soldiers cutting off the ears of their victims as trophies, of diseased and filthy concentration camps.

Appeals to American honor and sympathy for the underdog: Hearst repeatedly reminded Americans of their own rebellion against England, and of Cuba's being a tiny island

44

fighting against a great European power.

Then, on February 15, 1896, the American battleship *Maine* was sunk in Havana harbor. No one has ever discovered how the *Maine* was sunk. There is strong evidence that the Cubans, not the Spanish, were responsible. But the *Journal* did not seek proof or await results of an investigation. It used Misleading Association and pro-war Emotional Appeals. As soon as the news of the sinking arrived, *Journal* headlines screamed: "Destruction of the warship *Maine* was the work of an enemy"—and the newspaper made clear that by enemy it meant Spain. A few days later, even though the United States government did not declare war until April, the *Journal* headlines read, "The whole country thrills with war fever."

As the circulation of the *Journal* climbed to a million copies a day, other newspapers, such as the New York *World* and the *Sun,* hastened to jump on the propaganda bandwagon. While the Spanish government was still desperately trying to prove its innocence, Americans across the nation were shouting the *Journal*-inspired slogan "Remember the *Maine!*"

One point embedded in the propaganda was true enough: the Spanish colonies did want freedom. But Hearst, followed by other newspaper publishers, had deliberately incited the American public into believing that Spain was an enemy of the United States and a cruel imperialist. The result was the Spanish-American War, which the United States had no difficulty in winning quickly.

The *Journal*'s war propaganda had been circulation building, blatant, contrived and often falsified. Note, however, that the propaganda would not have succeeded so well if the American people of the time had not wanted it to succeed. The United States in the late 1890's was ripe for such a war, eager to show that it was a world power to be reckoned with—as Spain was not. Many Americans of the day believed in another popular slogan, "Manifest Destiny"— implying that it was the destiny of the United States to dominate the entire western hemisphere. The newspaper propaganda helped justify the United States' entry into war and afterwards its taking over of some of Spain's possessions, the Philippines and Puerto Rico, and assuming economic control in Cuba.

History sometimes turns back upon itself. During the next war the same propaganda tactics Hearst had used to instigate the Spanish-American War twisted back against him and his newspaper. Like many other Americans, Hearst over the years became an isolationist, and isolationists believed that the United States should stay out of World War I. But events—and propaganda—decreed otherwise.

World War I, which began in Europe in August, 1914, was the first war in which full-scale use of propaganda was employed by all of the governments concerned. From the very beginning, both Germany and its opponent England wanted the neutral United States to be its ally. Both sides turned to propaganda to sway the American people.

Germany's most effective propaganda was channeled through German-American organizations and German businesses in the United States. Germany also attempted a few slanted short-wave broadcasts in the very new communication medium of radio. However, the German propaganda was much more limited, and much less effective than the British.

The British started with an advantage because they had cut the German Atlantic cable in August, 1914. Any cable news about the war originating in Germany and Austria had to go through London, where stories were slanted toward the British-Allied side before being sent on to the United States. Also, British and French propagandists early

STORMING OF THE CASTLE OF CHAPULTEPEC, BY THE AMERICAN ARMY UNDER GENERAL SCOTT, SEPT. 13, 1847.

Sketches and engravings like this of the Battle of Chapultepec appeared in many American newspapers. It was an American victory in the Mexican War in 1847, a war won by the United States. But the Mexican War revealed that American soldiers doubtful of their cause could be propagandized into fighting for the other side. Mexican propaganda offered the Appeals of land, honor, and common religions beliefs. *Library of Congress*

Aerial balloons, such as this one, were used in reconnoitering Confederate positions in the Civil War. They were also used to drop propaganda leaflets. But balloons had already been used to distribute leaflets much earlier in Europe during the Napoleonic wars. *Library of Congress*

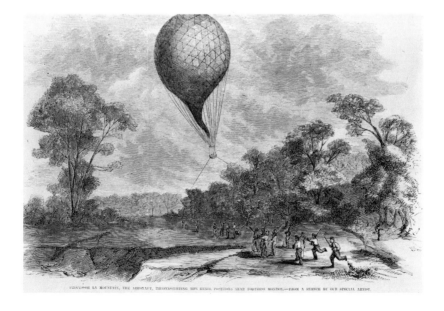

PROFESSOR LA MOUNTAIN, THE AERONAUT, RECONNOITERING THE REBEL POSITIONS NEAR FORTRESS MONROE.—FROM A SKETCH BY OUR SPECIAL ARTIST.

The efforts of Hearst's *New York Journal* to promote war with Spain are regarded as classic propaganda. This is the front page of the newspaper after the sinking of the U.S. battleship *Maine* in Havana harbor. *New York Journal, Feb. 17, 1898*

British and French propaganda of atrocities committed by German soldiers in the early years of World War I strongly influenced Americans and helped to bring about the United States' entry into the war on the side of the Allies. One of the better-known stories was of German soldiers chopping off a baby's hands during the "rape" of Belgium. Another "atrocity" story was the shooting down of a French boy, who had aimed his toy gun at Germans. Both atrocity stories were later admitted to be false. *Courtesy of* Look *magazine, June 18, 1938, and Library of Congress*

The "Remember the *Maine*" slogan in the Spanish-American War became "Remember the *Lusitania*" in World War I. The British passenger liner *Lusitania,* with 1,198 civilians aboard (124 Americans) was sunk in 1915 by a German submarine. Allied propaganda called submarine warfare "inhuman." Actually, both sides used submarines. Although the German ambassadorial type is wrapped in skull and crossbones here, the German Embassy did, in fact, warn Americans against sailing on British ships. *Library of Congress*

Without radio and television, the poster was an important instrument of mass persuasion in World War I. First Appeals were for recruitment in the United States, as in this Navy poster. It combines both a glamor and shame Appeal to eligible recruits. *St. Louis Public Library, St. Louis, Mo.*

Gee!! I Wish I Were a Man

I'd Join the Navy
Recruiting Station, 7th and Chestnut

After recruitment Appeals came Appeals to raise money to support World War I. This American poster used Glittering Generalities like "Liberty" bonds, as well as Fear Appeal. The archetypes of 100 percent good and 100 percent evil are clear. *St. Louis Public Library, St. Louis, Mo.*

(BELOW) Name Calling was another Appeal used in World War I posters to unite Americans behind the war. German soldiers were invariably referred to as "Huns"—meaning barbarians capable of savage cruelty, and depicted as gross, subhuman beasts. The Allied soldier was just as invariably depicted as clean-cut, brave, and noble. *U.S. War Department, Courtesy of National Archives*

This German Nazi propaganda poster reads "Who buys from the Jews is a traitor." Hitler needed a scapegoat to charge with Germany's troubles and the losing of World War I. A scapegoat also enabled Hitler to appear a hero for overcoming this "villain." The Jewish people, a minority in Germany, could not fight back effectively against this viciously directed propaganda. Hitler's Nazi regime controlled all mass communication in Germany. *Wiener Library, London, England*

Nazi German leaflet dropped on France in World War II, 1940. It says, "If you fight England's battle, your soldiers will fall like autumn leaves." *Froben Press*

This American "newspaper," distributed to German front-line soldiers in World War II, called attention to the numbers of Germans becoming prisoners of war and to new German defeats. *Paul M. A. Linebarger*

World War II German "radio" leaflet which invited Americans at Anzio in 1944 to surrender. This leaflet offered the use of German radio to transmit word to families that the surrendering soldiers were safe. *Paul M. A. Linebarger*

AMERICAN SOLDIERS!

Remember those happy days when you stepped out with your best girl "going places and doing things"?

No matter

whether you two were enjoying a nice juicy steak at some tony restaurant or watching a thrilling movie with your favourite stars performing, or dancing to the lilt of a swing band

you were happy.

WHAT IS LEFT OF ALL THIS?

Nothing! Nothing but days and nights of the heaviest fighting and for many of you

NOTHING BUT A PLAIN WOODEN CROSS IN FOREIGN SOIL!

FILL IN THIS BLANK AND KEEP IT

USE BLOCK LETTERS.

TO BE TRANSMITTED BY JERRY'S FRONT RADIO:

Name: _____

Rank: _____

Serial Number: _____

Address: _____ Street

Town: _____

Country: _____

In this panel write a short message of not more than 15 words which will be transmitted by radio

To the

German woman !

Germany herself will now be the Theater of War. Every bomb and every shell from now on will explode on German soil. German blood will sink into the German earth. Cities, villages and fields will go up in smoke and flames. Such is the wish of Hitler and his Party fanatics.

Do you want the war at home ?

Ask the returning German soldier

> whether individual bravery and courage can bring to a stop the Anglo-American war machine.

Ask the returning German soldier

> if he wants for German women and children the same fate that befell the civil population of Normandy, Italy and Russia.

Ask the returning German soldier

> if he wishes his country to look as do the shattered cities of Normandy, Italy and Russia.

The loyalty of the German soldier does not belong to the bankrupt Party but to you, German woman, to your children and your country. And you can save the German soldier, your children and your country from senseless destruction if you demand :

THE END !

Translation of American propaganda used in World War II to appeal to German women to stop the war. Appeals were to safety of family and country and against Nazi party "fanatics." The point was to encourage surrender, not only of civilians but of soldiers with whom the civilians were in contact. *U.S. Department of the Army, Psychological Operations*

HIS IS THE ENEMY

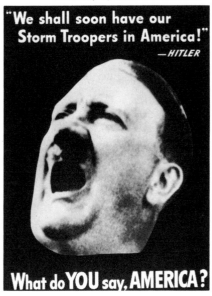

"We shall soon have our
Storm Troopers in America!"
—HITLER

What do YOU say, AMERICA?

This is the Enemy

Posters, as pictorial propaganda, were also used extensively in World War II for recruitment, raising money, and most important, to unite the American people against a common foe—The Enemy—in the above posters, Nazi Germany.

In World War II, Japanese propagandists dropped this leaflet on Australian troops stationed on lonely Pacific Islands while American troops were stationed in great numbers in Australia. The point was to arouse ill feeling between American and Australian forces, and to arouse Australian soldiers' fears of what was happening with their women "back home." The propaganda idea was very old: divide and conquer. *Marine Corps Museum, Quantico, Virginia*

Seeds were dropped on Burma with this Allied World War II leaflet. The idea was to show the Burmese people that the Japanese forces brought destruction and ruin, but "Wherever the Allied forces come, the fields spring up green." Information was given on how to sow the seeds. *Froben Press*

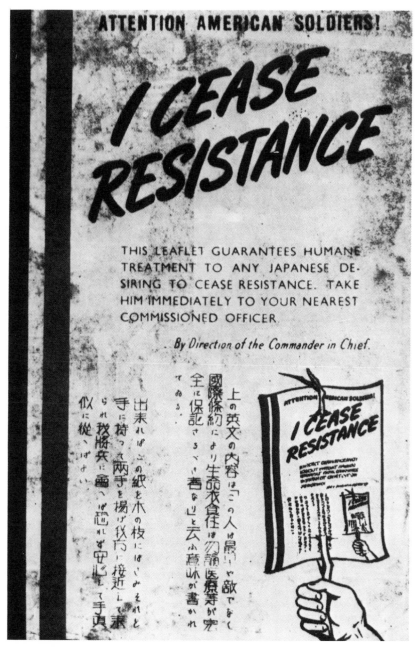

This American surrender leaflet was dropped on Japanese troops during World War II. Pictured clearly is how the Japanese soldier should put the leaflet on a stick so he will not be suspected of holding the leaflet over a hand grenade. Note that the wording used is the face-saving, "I cease resistance," rather than "I surrender." *Paul M. A. Linebarger*

turned to the use of such atrocity stories as the "Hun barbarians" (German soldiers) cutting off the hands of Belgian children, murdering women and babies and making soap out of dead soldiers. Although, after the war, British and French officials admitted these stories were deliberately and completely invented, they are still believed by some elderly Americans today.

Yet, not all the horror had to be invented. England's lifeline was the sea, and the German navy could not hope to stop British navy and supply ships, except by submarine —a new, unfamiliar and therefore horrifying means of warfare. German officials carefully warned Americans against traveling on Allied ships. But 114 Americans sailed on the British commercial liner *Lusitania,* and the ship was sunk by a German submarine. British propagandists skillfully exploited the sinking until "Remember the *Lusitania*" became as strong an American rallying cry and Slogan against Germany as "Remember the *Maine*" had been against Spain.

The United States declared war against Germany on April 6, 1917. Two weeks later, President Wilson set up the Committee of Public Information (CPI) to be run by George Creel. Creel's job—the first time in American history that any man had officially been given this power—was to coordinate government propaganda and to act as liaison between news outlets and the government. Creel saw his mission correctly as that of "fighting for the minds of men."

Soon, American propaganda leaflets began appearing in German trenches, aimed at demoralizing German troops, already weary from three years of warfare. One of the most effective leaflets, printed in German on a copy of the German Army's field postcard, was called the Invitation to Breakfast. Translated, the card read:

(Address side of postcard)

WRITE THE ADDRESS OF YOUR FAMILY UPON THIS CARD AND IF YOU ARE CAPTURED BY THE AMERICANS, GIVE IT TO THE FIRST OFFICER WHO QUESTIONS YOU. HE WILL MAKE IT HIS BUSINESS TO FORWARD IT IN ORDER THAT YOUR FAMILY MAY BE REASSURED CONCERNING YOUR SITUATION.

(Reverse side of postcard)

DO NOT WORRY ABOUT ME. THE WAR IS OVER FOR ME. I HAVE GOOD FOOD. THE AMERICAN ARMY GIVES ITS PRISONERS THE SAME FOOD AS ITS OWN SOLDIERS: BEEF, WHITE BREAD, POTATOES, BEANS, PRUNES, COFFEE, BUTTER, TOBACCO, ETC.

The Invitation to Breakfast postcard was used, and when it was sent home to Germany, it also helped lower German civilian morale. The German army finally began to pay its soldiers a few German marks for each of these "postcards" turned in.

So effective were American and other Allied propaganda leaflets that after the Battle of the Meuse-Argonne, it was found that one out of every three German prisoners had Allied propaganda leaflets hidden in a pocket or shoe. The German General Ludendorff in his war memoirs wrote, "We were hypnotized by the enemy propaganda as a rabbit by a snake. It was exceptionally clever and conceived on a great scale. It worked by strong mass suggestion, kept in closest touch with the military situation, and was unscrupulous as to the means it used."

Although American propaganda played its part in this overseas effort, the main job of the Committee of Public Information was not to spread its propaganda overseas, however, but to sell the war to the American people at home. Congress had passed the declaration of war, but there were still many people in the country who doubted the wisdom of America's entrance into the war. And in order for a democracy to wage war successfully, to recruit the large army necessary, and to raise funds from private citizens to support this army, it is essential that the government have the support of a thoroughly aroused public. It was Creel's job to convince the American people that the "American case for war against Germany was unimpeachable."

To complete this task, Creel used all his skills as a journalist, publicist and salesman—as well as the skills of scores of artists, actors, advertisers, writers, civic groups and professors. Editorials in favor of the war, written and distributed by the CPI, were printed by the thousands in newspapers and magazines. Special "Red, White and Blue" books were written by the CPI explaining the war to the American people.

Creel was particularly adept at seizing on memorable rallying Slogans like "The war to end wars" and "The war to make the world safe for democracy." These over-simplified Slogans, with emotional appeal but little specific meaning, convinced many Americans that the war was a holy crusade and worth any sacrifice.

Throughout the country, 75,000 anonymous Americans were organized as "four-minute men." In movie theaters, clubs, schools, wherever people gathered these four-minute men were ready to give a four-minute speech slanted strongly in favor of the war.

But the most important instrument of mass communication used by the CPI to promote the war was the poster. Long accepted as an inexpensive but effective medium of mass persuasion, in World War I the poster came into its own. It became a vital weapon in the hands of the propagandists. The war poster, which is simply pictorial propaganda, had a threefold mission: to stimulate patriotism and support for the war; to arouse hatred against a common enemy; and to raise money for liberty loans and various other financial "drives" necessary to winning the war.

These posters, which appeared all over the United States —on billboards, in shop windows, railroad stations, magazines and newspapers—utilized all the basic propaganda devices, including emotional Appeals to patriotism, duty, shame and fear. Posters exploited the atrocities of the enemy. The sinking of the *Lusitania* appeared in an unforgettable poster showing a mother drowning with a baby clutched in her arms; the one word on the poster was ENLIST. The enemy soldier was invariably Name-called "the Hun" and was shown as a beast in a spiked helmet, blood dripping from his knife, usually threatening a helpless woman or child. The Allied soldier was just as invariably cleancut, compassionate and noble.

By the end of the war, the American people had been saturated with government war propaganda. Probably never before or since has our government used propaganda as successfully as it did during the first world war. Creel's success, however, was helped along by two new United States laws: the Espionage Act of 1917 and the Sedition Act of 1918. These laws prevented criticism of the war from appearing in publications, on penalty of heavy fines and imprisonment. Only favorable views of the war were allowed to be printed. So effective was this control in uniting Americans behind the war that when William Randolph Hearst, who had opposed America's entry into this war, attempted to present both German and British viewpoints in his *Journal,* he was hanged in effigy, his paper boycotted and he, himself, denounced as a traitor.

It was perhaps as much because of these laws as because

once the war was over, many people realized they had been deliberately whipped into war hysteria by propaganda, that the Committee of Public Information fell into disfavor and was abolished in 1919. It took another twenty-three years, until June, 1942, for propaganda once more to become an official function of the United States government. World War II had arrived. This time, the propaganda agency was called the Office of War Information (OWI) and was under the direction of the well-known journalist Elmer Davis. Its overseas division was directed by the famous playwright Robert Sherwood. It is interesting to note that neither in World War I or II was "propaganda" mentioned in the titles of these governmental organizations.

But propaganda—no matter what it was called—in World War II was acknowledged to be an essential part of government. In Great Britain, the head of the propaganda organization was given cabinet rank. And in Germany, the Minister of Propaganda, Paul Joseph Goebbels, was second in power only to Adolf Hitler himself.

Hitler had been a corporal in World War I and had seen at firsthand propaganda's role in defeating Germany in that war. He had learned that "propaganda could be a truly frightening weapon in the hands of an expert." He made it exactly that. The history of propaganda in Nazi Germany under Hitler and his handpicked propaganda chief, Goebbels, would require several books. In a few short years, Nazi propaganda indoctrinated the German people into a belief that they were an invincible master race, and he, Hitler, was their predestined leader.

To gain power in Germany and in other countries during World War II, Hitler and Goebbels used all of the propaganda devices, but the three they found most useful and effective were the following:

The Scapegoat: The Jewish people were selected to be

blamed for all that had gone wrong in Germany, including the defeat in World War I. Hitler was the hero who would save Germans from further Jewish "wrongs."

Over-simplified Stereotypes: The Nazi Nordic Superman who would and should "rule for a thousand years."

Appeal to hatred and fear: Repeated highly emotional appeals to arouse hatred of other countries and other people.

The propaganda was backed up with terror, intimidation and complete government monopoly of information, which prevented the German people from hearing any other viewpoints.

Hitler's propaganda was equally effective in spreading disunity and fear among his enemies. Through propaganda leaflets and bombastic radio broadcasts it destroyed the will of a country like France to fight, before it was even attacked.

It was this Nazi propaganda machine, the most powerful yet known in the world, that the newly created Office of War Information of the United States had to face. To fight this war of words, as deadly in its own way as the war of guns, the Office of War Information used primarily three media: the age-old propaganda leaflet, the loudspeaker, and the radio. For the first time in American military history, a special military organization called the Psychological Warfare Division was created to use these weapons.

The soldiers of the psywar units were unlike any frontline combat soldiers ever seen before. Instead of guns and ammunition, they carried public address systems, radios, loudspeakers, typewriters and portable printing presses. Their missions ranged from massive leaflet airdrops over enemy lines, to a solitary sergeant driving within a thousand yards of an enemy position, and, over a loudspeaker mounted on his truck, calling out various appeals to prevail upon the enemy soldiers to surrender.

Hardened combat troops at first dubbed the Psywar units "feather merchants" or "confetti soldiers" and the loudspeakers, "hog-callers." Then, during the North African and Italian invasions and in the Normandy landings, when platoons of German and Italian soldiers began coming in with arms raised, in response to the "hog-callers," the combat soldiers changed their minds. Even General George Patton came to approve and asked to have the Psywar loudspeakers placed on his forward tanks. With improved amplifiers that achieved a range of two miles, the loudspeakers also aided in mopping up operations on Okinawa and other Pacific Islands. There, fanatic Japanese dug in for a last-ditch stand were persuaded to live rather than die for their emperor.

Propaganda leaflets proved equally useful in persuading the enemy to surrender. Over eight billion leaflets were dropped in the European and Mediterranean theater alone. Twenty-seven million leaflets were dropped along the invasion coast on D-Day. In August and September of 1944 a survey disclosed that 25 percent of the German soldiers taken prisoner were deserters, and 90 percent of them had American propaganda leaflets in their possession.

These leaflets included white, black, and gray propaganda. The colors do not refer to the color of the paper used. White propaganda gives the real origin of the propaganda. Black propaganda pretends to be from the enemy's own sources. One of the most interesting examples of black propaganda in World War II was a booklet printed by the OWI and distributed behind German lines. Disguised as an official German medical handbook, the booklet actually taught German soldiers how to pretend illness to get out of active duty!

Perhaps the most useful gray propaganda items—which show no source at all—were the American-printed newspapers and news notes dropped or scattered over enemy lines. The German soldiers undoubtedly suspected the source of these newspapers, but they were so hungry for news they read them anyway. In fact, they occasionally complained when issues were missed!

But most successful of all, in this combat of words, was a comparatively new propaganda tool, radio. More than two-thirds of the OWI's budget was concentrated on its radio operations, and both white and black propaganda were used. White propaganda, as the Voice of America, attempted to tell the enemy listeners the truth and gave its official source. Black propaganda often pretended to come from secret German stations; the purpose of these broadcasts was to confuse and mislead the enemy.

Hitler recognized the damage that these Allied broadcasts were doing, by breaking through the wall of lies he had built around the German people. Unsuccessful attempts were made to jam the air channels, and the growing number of Germans who listened secretly to these Allied broadcasts were threatened with imprisonment and death. The Gestapo even spread the rumor that it had a secret invention that could detect anyone listening to these forbidden radio broadcasts! Goebbels called these BBC and American broadcasts "poison for the German people concealed behind a mask of objective sounding news items and comments."

As more and more of the German people and German soldiers began hearing the Allied broadcasts and propaganda appeals, Hitler's use of the "big lie" began to react against him, at least militarily. His soldiers began to crack. But so strong was Hitler's hold over the minds and emotions of the German people that it wasn't until the German troops were utterly defeated, that the whole Nazi façade crumbled.

United States psychological warfare operations undoubtedly helped to hasten the German defeat and certainly lessened the number of casualties for both sides in the conflict.

But our propaganda was never as extensive as Nazi Germany's, nor was psywar a miracle worker—just another kind of weapon, effective under the right conditions.

Despite its obvious successes in the field, the Office of War Information was subject to constant criticism during the war from both the United States Congress and the people, because Americans still feared and distrusted propaganda. At one time, it took the intervention of General Eisenhower and General McClure, both well aware of the importance of psychological warfare operations, to save the OWI from a sudden drastic budget cut. After the war ended, the OWI, like Creel's Committee on Public Information, was quickly abolished, for most Americans had yet to learn that propaganda cannot be abolished as long as war—and human nature—exists.

And wars, in Korea and Vietnam, came. They only pointed up more clearly the truth of General Eisenhower's statement that "Psychological warfare has proven its right to a place of dignity in our military arsenal." Eventually the role of propaganda as a weapon was no longer questioned, not in Korea and not in Vietnam. What began to be questioned was just how big and how important that role should be in determining war—and peace.

War Propaganda in Korea and Vietnam: East Meets West

IT WAS the desperate summer and early fall of 1950. North Korean Communist troops, without warning, had crossed the United Nations-made borderline and had swarmed down on South Korea. The surprise was complete. United States occupation troops, rushed frantically to South Korea's aid from nearby Japan and Okinawa, were outnumbered and in large part ill-equipped and unprepared. With their advantage of surprise, the North Koreans quickly pushed back the South Korean and United States troops, down toward Pusan and the sea. It was only a matter of time before North Korean victory and take-over was assured.

Time was what was needed: for the United States to send in divisions of trained troops and to request and receive

United Nations troop aid for South Korea. To get that time, the advance of the North Korean troops had to be slowed down.

The time was bought by the sacrificial fighting of American and South Korean troops and by the heroic stand they made at the Pusan perimeter. The time was bought also, in part, by American propaganda.

To delay the North Korean soldiers, a billion leaflets were dropped by American propagandists. The first used the Appeal of Fear, playing on the one strength the United States had in Korea—control of the air. The idea was to make the North Korean soldier even more fearful than he already was of United States planes and induce him to dig in whenever planes were sighted—thereby slowing down the soldier's swift advance toward the sea.

The time was gained. North Korean soldiers began to take cover whenever American planes of any type appeared. The needed support from the United States and the United Nations came before the Pusan defenders were pushed into the sea. With newly added manpower and more equipment, the United Nations forces pushed the North Koreans steadily back. With the change in the balance of power came a change in propaganda. American psywar units, largely deactivated after World War II but once more active, prepared conventional surrender safe-conduct leaflets and dropped them from the air and shot them in mortar shells into North Korean lines. The pamphlets included such appeals to incite surrender as the promise of cigarettes, food and medical attention. But when the almost victorious United States troops and their allies reached the North Korean-Chinese border in the Christmas season of 1950, they suddenly faced an entirely new foe.

Until then—with the war a half-year old—the North Koreans had been helped only by Soviet and Chinese advisors and equipment. Now, divisions of Chinese troops crossed the border and flung themselves on the United Nations forces. Once again surprised, the United Nations forces suffered grievous losses and retreated toward central Korea. Here the fighting steadied.

During this period, American propagandists tried to lower North Korean morale by arousing suspicion of Chinese and Russian intentions. The Americans also called the attention of North Korean and Chinese soldiers to the neglect they suffered, compared with the South Korean soldiers who received good medical care and material support. But the most spectacular propaganda effort by Americans—using leaflets, newspapers, radio and loudspeakers—came near the end of the Korean War. The propaganda appeal used was an old one: money, if the enemy soldier would desert.

The Appeal—in Russian, Chinese and Korean—was addressed to any "courageous jet pilot" on the Communist side, offering, "if you like freedom . . . if you have courage . . . if you want to live a better, honorable life . . . fly a MIG combat airplane, intact, landing behind United Nations lines." The first deserting Communist pilot was promised $100,000; any following, $50,000.

A North Korean pilot did accept this propaganda appeal and defected with his MIG fighter plane. Not only was it the first combat MIG, undamaged, that the United States had been able to examine at close range, but, because of the defection, the Communists grounded all MIG's for more than a week. Also, for the ninety days that followed, either North Korean pilot morale was lowered, or some of the better North Korean pilots remained grounded. During this period, American Sabres destroyed 165 MIG's with only 3 combat losses—an unheard of ratio of 55–1 in favor of the United Nations pilots.

Effective as the American psywar effort was in the Korean War, however, there can be little doubt that the North Koreans, aided by the Chinese and the Soviet Communists, were the victors in propaganda. The Communist propaganda in Korea ranged from one of the oldest, most primitive forms of propaganda to a modern media, world-wide campaign that *Fortune* magazine said, "must be put down as Stalin's final masterpiece in the fabric of history."

The primitive propaganda appeared during the fiercely cold Korean winter nights of 1950–51. American soldiers, ordered not to zip up their sleeping bags because too many of them had been caught in them when the Chinese attacked, felt the cold and the snow and slept fitfully.

Then, with shocking abruptness, dozens of shrill bugles blared over loudspeakers, cymbals clashed, high menacing screams leaped out of the darkness. For only moments—but vital moments—the weird sounds paralyzed, panicked and confused the awakened Americans. Those moments gave the Chinese time to complete their "human wave" attacks.

Just sound? Yes, the oldest form of war propaganda. When used as Sun Tzu, the Chinese military genius of the fifth century B.C., suggested, sound can be used as a propaganda Appeal to Fear, confusing the enemy and destroying his will to fight—*before* the battle begins.

In leaflets, radio broadcasts and over loudspeakers, the Communists used more routine modern psychological warfare against American and United Nations forces.

These, no doubt, had their effect on soldiers, but the greatest propaganda success of Communism in Korea had an influence on peoples throughout the world. This propaganda effort was aided by war conditions, and although North Koreans and Chinese Communists supported what was a unique campaign, Soviet Russia is generally credited with most of the work. Basically, this world-wide propaganda campaign was one giant atrocity story—an appeal to the world's horror at the United States' use of "germ warfare" in Korea.

In 1952, Communist news media deluged the world with the news that United States forces were depositing germladen crackers, spiders, insects, leaves, pork and goose feathers in order to spread cholera, typhus and the plague in North Korea. Under wartime conditions and with poor sanitation, these diseases did exist in North Korea. Communist scientific "experts" were quoted to support the guilt of the Americans, and "confessions" from American prisoners were used. One American pilot, in a widely distributed tape recording, admitted, "These war mongers from Wall Street compelled me to commit a terrible crime against a people—to drop germ bombs on a peace loving population." At European conferences and at the United Nations, Communist officials accused the United States of waging germ warfare.

Although the United States asked for an impartial United Nations or Red Cross investigation of the charges, the Communists refused to allow either to enter North Korea. Fantastic though this unsupported propaganda may seem, it was believed by many people throughout the world—and is still believed.

Perhaps more shocking to the American military, after the war had been brought to a truce, was the discovery that the Communists had also won another kind of propaganda victory in the Korean War. In an impartial study made by Eugene Kinkead of American prisoners of war in Korea, it was disclosed that one out of every three American prisoners had in some degree cooperated or collaborated with the enemy during imprisonment. Admittedly, prisoners were subjected to brainwashing and intimidation, but British and Turkish prisoners had stood firm and American prisoners had not. Also, twenty-one American prisoners of war had

71

refused repatriation, preferring to remain with the Communists. (Many later changed their minds.) The question had to be rasied: To what extent had Communist propaganda influenced these American soldiers before and after capture? Why had Americans been most susceptible?

Whatever the reasons, the United States military began looking for ways and means of educating American soldiers to withstand enemy propaganda and intimidation, as well as taking steps to improve its own use of propaganda in wartime. When the United States became involved in another land war in Asia, this time in South Vietnam, psychological warfare units arrived in Saigon along with the first big contingents of American troops.

These psychological warfare units brought with them the most modern psychological warfare equipment. Portable printing presses that could turn out a million leaflets a day, used paper of special weight and size that would pack into specially fused aerial bombs. These bombs could scatter leaflets as much as a hundred miles away. New U-10 psychological warfare monoplanes were equipped with wings and landing gear specifically designed for leaflet dropping. Aerial loudspeakers attached to C-54's provided a means for broadcasting propaganda from the air. Yet, as modern as the equipment was, the propaganda devices used in the leaflets and the broadcasts were the old ones.

Other approaches such as Appeal to Superstitions, continued to be used. An ace of spades, like those in plastic playing cards, was left beside bodies of dead Viet Cong or dropped along Viet Cong trails to arouse Viet Cong fears that death surely followed the deadly omen. More direct approaches were made by loudspeaker airplanes that, in daily trips over Communist strongholds, boomed out recordings of crying babies or weeping women with the announcer asking: "Is this your child? Is this your wife? If so, what are

One of the many American propaganda leaflets designed to make North Korean soldiers fearful and dig in under American air power. The idea behind these leaflets was to slow down the North Korean ground advance. *Paul M. A. Linebarger*

'Rotation' isn't going to get you out of this war.

'Rotation' is only a new trick by those big shots back in the States to keep you fighting.

There've been 226,000 casualties in Korea already. 'Rotation' isn't going to save you because you may be 'rotated' back.

You have to risk your life for a nine-month period in Korea before it comes to your turn. Even if you are lucky enough to quit Korea alive, that's temporary. According to AP despatch on Sept. 15, 400 veterans of the 34th regiment were sent back to Korea from Japan on August 29 and have been reorganized into the 14th regiment. It is clear that as long as the war continues, mutilation and death are your constant companions.

Most GIs see through this rotation trick. Wise GIs know that only peace and a live-and-let-live attitude by all nations in the world can avoid death and suffering.

North Korean propaganda leaflet aimed at American soldiers in the Korean War, 1951. *Michael Choukas,* Propaganda Comes of Age *(Public Affairs Press)*

North Korean propaganda used quotes from American sources to support statements aimed at destroying American soldiers' willingness to fight. *Marine Corps Museum, Quantico, Virginia*

USE YOUR HEAD, SOLDIER!
If You Want to Keep It!

Associated Press reported from Seoul, October 8:

"North Korean artillery fired 39,000 rounds within 24 hours ending 6 o'clock October 7. Soldiers were pinned down for long hours in the trenches and bunkers by enemy fire which continued for days and nights."

Hanson Baldwin, *New York Times* military commentator wrote June 12:

"Superiority on the battlefront, which the UN had a year ago, has now moved to the enemy side."

U.S. News & World Report wrote June 21:

"U.S. air superiority in Korea is no longer absolute."

EVERY G.I. THAT'S BEEN IN BATTLE KNOWS THE SCORE:

● Bullets and shells hit everything above ground. He's smart to get in a hole and stay there.
● To go out on patrol is the best way to get killed. Don't do it.
● The first man forward in an assault is the first man to get hit. What's the good of looking for death?

USE YOUR HEAD AND PLAY SAFE!

The "divide and conquer" approach in American propaganda in Korea. This leaflet shows the North Korean soldier being pushed to the war front by the Chinese and the Russian Communists. The North Korean soldiers were the ones doing most of the fighting. *Marine Corps Museum, Quantico, Virginia*

American propaganda in the Korean War. Chinese military hand held over North Korean soldier's eyes to prevent him from seeing United Nations facts on Korean War. The leaflets distributed to North Korean forces were aimed at splitting up the Chinese and North Korean alliance. *Marine Corps Museum, Quantico, Virginia*

EI$ENHOWER, INC.

IKE PROMISED PEACE TO GET ELECT-ED, BUT HE HAS SOLD YOU OUT TO BIG BUSINESS!

BIG BUSINESS WON'T BRING PEACE BECAUSE IT MAKES BILLIONS OUT OF THE WAR.

Do you doubt this? Just look at Ike's Cabinet.

Dulles

Secretary of State:

JOHN FOSTER DULLES, Rockefeller corporation lawyer, connected with the International Nickel Co. which makes plenty out of munitions, the man who helped start the Korean war under Truman.

Wilson

Secretary of Defence:

CHARLES E. WILSON, president of General Motors, the nation's biggest war contractor. Picking Wilson, Ike said cynically that he wanted to "get a business brain in a $60-billion business" (i.e. the Defence Dept.). *Time* magazine, Dec. 1, 1952.

Secretary of the Army:

ROBERT TEN BROECK STEVENS, director of General Electric Co. and General Food Corp. (He makes money out of your rations.)

Secretary of the Navy:

ROBERT B. ANDERSON, vice-president of Associated Refineries (oil men do pretty well out of war too.)

This gang is so bad that even Senator Wayne Morse of Oregon, himself a Republican, has appealed to the people to "check the reactionary plunderers before they get started."

AMERICAN SOLDIERS!

IT'S BUSINESS FOR THEM—BUT IT'S WAR AND DEATH FOR YOU!

EISENHOWER WON'T GET YOU OUT OF THIS MESS—OUT OF THIS SENSELESS WAR.

ONLY IF THE PEOPLES THROUGHOUT THE WORLD GET TOGETHER FOR PEACE, PEACE CAN BE WON.

North Korean and Chinese propaganda in the Korean War directed against American soldiers, appealing to their fears of being victimized and dying for profiteers in the United States. The attack is really on American soldiers' morale. *Marine Corps Museum, Quantico, Virginia*

Two sides of Chinese safe-conduct pass offered to American soldiers in Korean War, with Appeals of safety and medical treatment. On the opposite side is a Bandwagon Appeal, "Thousands have done it . . ." *Marine Corps Museum, Quantico, Virginia*

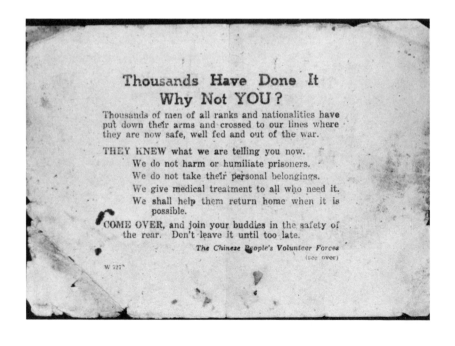

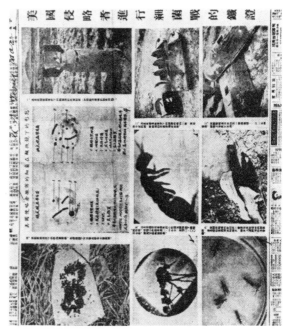

View of page of Communist newspaper, *Peking People's Daily,* March 15, 1952, accusing the United States of bombarding North Korea and China with insects that would spread disease. The pictures, impressive to the uninformed, were actually of ordinary flies, mosquitoes, and harmless bacteria. The bomb fragments shown (extreme right) are of bombs that carry propaganda leaflets but could not possibly carry germs. *Life magazine*

The French pro-Communist newspaper *Ce Soir,* April, 1952, copied the Peking germ-warfare propaganda and added pictures of angry-looking but common Asian flies. The *Ce Soir* headline reads, "United States Bacteriological War on Korea and China. These documents accuse." What the propagandists did not mention, of course, was that Communist powers refused to allow the International Red Cross to investigate the accusations. *Life magazine*

The cartoon by Fitzpatrick shows the Communist propagandist blasting out continually the "same old germ-warfare bug." Although few Americans believed the germ-warfare propaganda, people in many other countries did. *Fitzpatrick*, St. Louis Post Dispatch

SAME OLD PROPAGANDA BUG

ST. LOUIS POST-DISPATCH

In low-altitude airdrops, chutes can be used from the airplane to drop leaflets. This method has been used since World War I. Two men can dispense thousands of leaflets per minute using this technique. *Department of the Army, Psychological Operations*

The M129 leaflet bomb being prepared here can carry 30,000 leaflets. A fuse detonates, detaching the fins and releasing the leaflets. Depending on the wind and other factors, the leaflets may drift from almost a half mile to more than a mile. *Department of the Army, Psychological Operations*

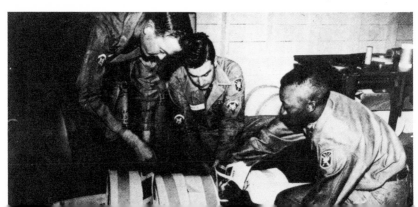

SAFE-CONDUCT PASS TO BE HONORED BY ALL VIETNAMESE GOVERNMENT AGENCIES AND ALLIED FORCES

Đây là một tấm Giấy Thông Hành có giá trị với tất cả cơ quan Quân Chính Việt - Nam Cộng - Hòa và lực lượng Đồng - Minh.

№ 665582 BT

이 안전보장패쓰는 월남정부와 모든 연합군에 의해 인정된 것입니다.

ĐÂY TẤM GIẤY THÔNG HÀNH CÓ GIÁ TRỊ VỚI TẤT CẢ CƠ - QUAN QUÂN CHÍNH VIỆT - NAM CỘNG - HÒA VÀ LỰC - LƯỢNG ĐỒNG - MINH.
SAFE-CONDUCT PASS TO BE HONORED BY ALL VIETNAMESE GOVERNMENT AGENCIES AND ALLIED FORCES
이 안전보장패쓰는 월남정부와 모든 연합군에 의해 인정된 것입니다.

American safe-conduct (surrender) passes for North Vietnamese or Viet Cong soldiers. The safe-conduct passes are made as official in appearance as possible, complete with official numbers. Appeal is directed toward women to pass on these passes "more valuable than gold," because they can save the lives of their men. The passes offer safety, good treatment, and, as pictured, friendship. *Department of the Army, Psychological Operations*

This American counterfeit of a North Vietnamese one-dong note was dropped to North Vietnamese villagers and troops. Words on the reverse of the note translate: "Money is worth less and less. As the war goes on, there will be less and less to buy. Prices will go higher and higher. Your savings will become worthless papers." *Department of the Army, Psychological Operations*

79

This American leaflet addressed to Viet Cong and North Vietnamese Communist soldiers asks, "Are you starving?" A translation reads: "We know you are hiding in the forests, clinging to a hopeless cause while you starve to death. Your leaders have deserted you; your friends have been killed; you are alone. Why continue this miserable life? Surrender to the South Vietnamese government forces. You will be well-treated and will receive food and medical care." *Department of the Army, Psychological Operations*

Các bạn có đang bị đói không?
•#•

Cùng các bạn cán binh trong MTGPMN và Quân Đội Bắc-Việt!

Chúng tôi biết hiện các bạn đang trốn-tránh trong rừng sâu, cố bám vào một chủ-nghĩa vô-vong, trong khi các bạn đang bị đói và sắp chết. Các cấp chỉ-huy đã bỏ rơi các bạn. Các đồng-chí của các bạn đã bị giết. Các bạn đang bị đơn-độc. Tại sao phải tiếp-tục cuộc sống bi-đát này? Hãy hồi-chánh với Chánh-Phủ Quốc-Gia. Các bạn sẽ được tiếp-đón nồng-hậu, đối-đãi tử-tế, được cung-cấp lương-thực và được chăm sóc thuốc men đầy-đủ.
6-163-68

An American Chieu Hoi or "Open Arms" Appeal at the province of Tay Ninh, Vietnam. The poster and leaflets like it, distributed to the Viet Cong, offer the Appeals of safety, rehabilitation, and job training. Also being suggested, though unstated, is desertion. The poster, showing a returnee rejoining his family, states 2,271 Viet Cong have rallied to the government in Tay Ninh and are enjoying a life free from fear and deprivation. *Department of the Army, Psychological Operations*

CHIÊU HỒI-TÂY NINH

Hồi chánh viên trở về gia đình. ▶

Tại Tây Ninh tổng số hồi chánh viên là 2.271 người gồm đủ các thành phần như: Chính Quy, Du Kích, Đặc Công, Nông Hội, Kinh Tài, Tuyên Vân Giáo, Đảng Viên Cộng Sản, Đoàn Viên các tổ chức vận vân ... Những hồi chánh viên này đã mang về nhiều vũ khí, đạn dược và tài liệu quan trọng. Một số đông đã trở về sum họp với gia đình. Một số hiện phục vụ trong các cơ quan Chính phủ. Họ đã hưởng cảnh sống tự do, đầy đủ.

Two-sided American leaflet—one side has theme "Government Vietnamese and U.S. soldiers work to repair bridge." Added words translate: "The governments of South Vietnam and the United States are working together to rebuild the roads and bridges for the good people of South Vietnam. You can help your government by reporting all Viet Cong activity to the government officials."

The theme of the other side is "The Viet Cong bring death and destruction to Vietnam." Added words translate: "The Viet Cong have no concern for human life or for the good people of Vietnam. The Viet Cong are desperate because they are being beaten by the government." *Department of the Army, Psychological Operations*

Nguyen Van Be picture, of the type used in American leaflets, proving he was alive and had not died a "hero's" death as the North Vietnamese Communists had claimed. *Department of the Army, Psychological Operations*

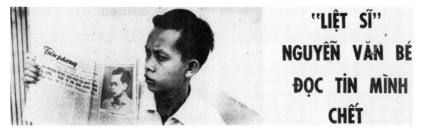

This Hanoi main-street scene shows North Vietnamese propaganda bill-boards with war scenes in the South. The slogan on the right states, "All out to defeat the American aggressors." An American plane shot down by heroic North Vietnamese figures can be seen in the center. The men in the foreground on the tracks are in a typical Vietnamese seated pose. *Marc Riboud Agence Magnum*

you, a North Vietnamese, fighting for in the South?" A new propaganda approach was the Chieu Hoi Amnesty leaflet. This was more than a safe-conduct leaflet. It also offered a new life and vocational training. Defectors were brought, as promised, to Chieu Hoi or Open Arms centers, where they were trained from six to twelve weeks in vocations and were lectured to for two hours daily on Communist versus democratic methods. Afterwards, those volunteering were placed in propaganda teams to go out into the villages and try to convert Viet Cong sympathizers.

These American propaganda efforts must have had at least a limited success because the Viet Cong began spreading rumors that American propaganda leaflets were poison-tipped and Viet Cong unit commanders were ordered to "take firm control of your troops" and diminish exposure to propaganda. "Cover your ears and shout" when loudspeaker planes appeared or "beat on pots and pans," they were ordered. Despite these attempts to blot out American and South Vietnamese propaganda, an American survey showed that a quarter of the North Vietnamese soldiers defecting said they were influenced by the leaflets, and even more carried the leaflets on them when they surrendered. Ho Chi Minh himself said in a speech before his death that, "we must further heighten our determination to smash all spying and psychological war activities of the enemy."

The Communist propagandists used many of the same approaches and devices. The Communists beamed out radio broadcasts and sent storytellers and players, as well as films, to villages, to tell their story of the war. They trained and used, much more effectively than the South Vietnamese or Americans, their own soldiers as propagandists skilled in person-to-person village propaganda. Admittedly, also, the Communists used terrorism—fear propaganda—to force village cooperation. But neither side was innocent of this.

Why then does the Communist propaganda seem to have been more effective—with the Vietnamese people and with the world's peoples? Were the Communist propagandists more skillful?

Not necessarily. The North Vietnamese propagandists had at least three great propaganda advantages, which they exploited repeatedly:

1. Americans were strangers—foreign devils. They could easily be pictured as the Stereotypes of white imperialists, the same as the hated French imperialists who had ruled Vietnam for one hundred years—until 1954.

2. Ho Chi Minh, leader of the North Vietnamese Communist regime, was the "George Washington" of Vietnam who had pushed out the French.

3. North Vietnam is a small underdeveloped country. It faced a big powerful United States. Thus, the Hanoi propaganda could and did stress the ever effective David and Goliath Appeal, the appeal of the underdog, the little guy fighting the big guy. Chinese and Russian aid was played down.

With the Vietnamese people themselves, the Communist propagandists sometimes used the David and Goliath approach with a foreign-devil twist. The following is a translation of one leaflet used:

THE PAPER GIANT

HIS HEAD IS A BLOCKHOUSE

HIS BEARD IS BARBED WIRE

HIS EYES ARE BOMBS

HIS TEETH ARE DUM DUM BULLETS

HIS TWO ARMS ARE GUNS

AND FROM HIS NOSE SQUIRT FLAMES

AS A VAMPIRE, HE SUCKS THE BLOOD OF LITTLE
CHILDREN

HIS FOREHEAD IS A NEST OF ARTILLERY
HIS BODY IS AN AIRFIELD
HIS FINGERS ARE BAYONETS, HIS FEET TANKS
HE PUTS OUT HIS FANGS IN ORDER TO THREATEN
BUT IN HIS HIDEOUS MOUTH HE CAN ONLY CHEW
SCRAP IRON BECAUSE HE HAS AGAINST HIM THE
POWERFUL HATRED OF OUR PEOPLE WHO ARE
FIGHTING VALIANTLY AGAINST IMPERIALIST
TYRANTS
ALL THINGS CONSIDERED, THE AMERICAN IS A
PAPER GIANT.

In Vietnam, the propaganda war for men's minds and loyalties had to be considered even more important in the long run than the military conflict. Both sides showed some awareness of this. As evidence, one incident can be cited of a struggle that was not over a soldier's life but over his "image."

In May, 1967, a twenty-one-year-old North Vietnamese Communist soldier named Nguyen Van Be was reported killed in action. He had, in Communist reports, voluntarily sacrificed his life by striking a mine detonator against an American armored vehicle, killing himself and "sixty-nine American aggressors and puppet troops." He had been a Revolutionary Youth party member, in frail health, and was the eldest son of a poor peasant family of the war-ravaged Mekong delta. He had been an ammunition carrier, the lowest rank for a soldier. His was a perfect hero "image," and Communist propagandists seized on it. Thousands of young men and women in Hanoi were given a six-week course on how to live up to the exploits of young Be. Communist teachers in North and South Vietnam were instructed to sing Be's story of sacrifice for the Communist cause. His image was admired by millions.

Then something went wrong. Nguyen Van Be turned up alive, captured and in custody of South Vietnamese government troops in Saigon. Gleefully, the United States and South Vietnamese propagandists broadcast the live Be's denial that he had done anything heroic. They dropped tens of millions of leaflets, including one of Be pictured holding a Hanoi newspaper that showed his photograph and obituary. The heroic image—and therefore by implication the Communist propaganda as well—was a lie.

Be, as a soldier, was not important to either side. It was his propaganda image that mattered. Communist propagandists denied the American and South Vietnamese broadcasts and leaflets and continued to insist that Nguyen Van Be had died with heroic sacrifice—as all good young Communists should believe themselves willing to do. American officials learned that the Viet Cong offered two million piasters (about $17,000) to anyone who killed Nguyen Van Be, and this was exploited. Before the young Be was finally allowed to drop into obscurity, more than fifty million leaflets about him had been dropped in North and South Vietnam, and great sums of money had been spent to build—and to destroy—not a soldier but his "image."

Of course, the Vietnamese Communist apparatus seized on the peace marches in the United States to impress both the Vietnamese and Americans in Vietnam with the "inevitable victory" for the "people's forces," and the faltering United States support. And American propagandists have hit at North Vietnamese hardships and weariness with war in "far-away" South Vietnam. But the inevitable question must be asked: Is it worthwhile—all the time, effort and money spent on psychological warfare?

From a cold-blooded financial viewpoint—yes. Official financial estimates are that it takes $100,000 to kill one Vietnamese Communist soldier. In one of the worst periods of the war, in December, 1966, the United States Air Force announced that 19,073 Communist soldiers had come in with Chieu Hoi leaflets, thus saving the United States $1,907,300,000.

From a less cold-blooded point of view, psychological warfare can be considered the most humane weapon of war. It saves lives rather than destroys them, in most cases. Thousands of Germans and Japanese are alive today because they believed American propaganda appeals and risked surrender in World War II. Also, thousands of Americans are alive who might have been killed by these enemy soldiers had they continued fighting. Of course, psychological warfare propaganda is only humane if the promises and appeals have some substance of truth.

The ancient Chinese General Sun Tzu pointed out in his book: "To win a hundred victories is not the acme of skill. To subdue the enemy without fighting is the acme of skill." As long as wars persist in human history, psychological warfare will be used. From Vietnam, perhaps more than any war in American history, emerges the even greater truth. It will be the nation or nations that master persuasion most completely that will win the last war—the battle, not for men's guns, but for men's minds.

Early American Political Propaganda: Log Cabin to White House

IN 1840, 80 percent of the voters of the United States—a higher percentage than ever before or ever since—turned out to elect a President. This unusual voter enthusiasm was aroused by a campaign that was more propaganda than politics.

The candidates were William Henry Harrison of the Whig party and Martin Van Buren of the Democrat party. Van Buren was running for his second term as President. He had been handpicked for his job by the popular Andrew Jackson, former President of the United States and leader of the Democrat party, known as the party of the common man. The less popular Whig party was regarded as the party of the aristocrats, of wealthy Southern planters and Eastern bankers. To add to its difficulties, the Whig party was split into many factions, unable to agree on its platform. With this weak opposition, Van Buren looked like a sure winner. He might have been—if it had not been for the propaganda use of Stereotype. The Stereotype won more of the early—and some not so early—American Presidential campaigns than any other propaganda approach. A stereotype is a fixed, over-simplified picture that people have of a certain "type" of person. (Some stereotypes in use today are hippy or Establishment square or Uncle Tom.) The individual may not fit into the stereotype at all; he may have entirely different qualities from his "type." But people of today, as in the past, see only his "type."

Even before 1840, American politicians could and did use the Stereotype—putting a candidate into a popular picture already existing in people's minds, a kind of pre-set image. In 1828, the Democrat party came to power by supporting Andrew Jackson as the general at the Battle of New Orleans and a backwoodsman; this put Jackson into the two most popular Stereotypes of the day: "war hero" and "log cabin man." (The "war hero" Stereotype presented a strong, courageous man who could not fail to lead his land to victory. The "log cabin" Stereotype presented an honest, plain-living, hard-working common man, born in a log cabin and not ashamed of it.)

The Whig leaders in 1840 cleverly decided to disavow their party's aristocratic character and to ignore the important national issues—on which they could not agree anyway—and instead appeal directly to voters' emotions. For the first time in America's political history, politicians built a whole political campaign around a stereotype. The voters liked a war hero? They'd give them a war hero. The voters liked a log cabin man? They'd give them a log cabin man.

From the beginning of the campaign, William Henry Harrison was presented as a simple farmer, a humble man of the people, who preferred a log cabin to a fancy home, and hard cider to expensive bourbon whisky. The log cabin, in fact, became the symbol of the Whig campaign. (The symbol can be important propagandically, because a picture can be taken in more quickly than words. It is an instant short cut to an emotional response on the part of the viewer.)

Handkerchiefs were imprinted with log cabins and handed out to voters. Log cabin songs were especially written for the campaign. Badges, hard-cider almanacs and posters picturing Harrison hard at work plowing on his farm or sitting before his log cabin were seen everywhere. Political parades and torchlight processions, stretching for miles, were held for Harrison all over the country. Floats on which actual log cabins had been built, with real smoke pouring out of the chimneys, were pulled down the street by perspiring men—the men wearing coonskin caps. Barrels of hard cider were prominently displayed, and their contents liberally dispensed to all at the massive political rallies that followed the parades.

In addition to his being presented in Stereotype picture as a plain log cabin man, Harrison was also presented in Stereotype picture as a "war hero" for his service in the Battle of Tippecanoe. The battle had occurred in 1811 against Indians in Florida, twenty-nine years before the Presidential campaign, but soon Harrison was being affectionately called "Old Tippecanoe." As the Vice-Presidential candidate was named John Tyler, the catchy campaign slogan, "Tippecanoe and Tyler, too," was on every tongue. Old Tippecanoe was shown in campaign posters in front of his log cabin offering jugs of hard cider to his old soldier-comrades.

.

Not only did the Whig politicians use a "good" Stereotype to influence voters in favor of their candidate, they used a "bad" Stereotype to influence voters against Van Buren. This Stereotype, too, was carefully chosen: the "hateful aristocrat," the effete man from the eastern seaboard that western frontiersmen and small town people of the 1840's instinctively distrusted and disliked.

To fit President Van Buren into this Stereotype, the propaganda devices of Name Calling and Ridicule were used. Van Buren was pictured in cartoons in newspapers and magazines as a conceited dandy, who laced himself into women's corsets and strutted around like a peacock. The use of political cartoons—which is simply another form of Name Calling—was, of course, not a new propaganda device in the 1840's. Political cartoons to ridicule an opposing candidate and therefore influence voters against him had been used in political campaigns since colonial days.

To add to the detested "aristocrat" Stereotype, Whig Representative Charles Ogle, in a speech before the House of Representatives, accused President Van Buren of turning the White House into a royal palace, spending money lavishly on new decorations and furniture, and eating French food from golden plates while the common people starved. The speech was filled with the propaganda word devices of Name Calling, Loaded Words and Glittering Generalities —as well as bald-faced lies—but it was widely reprinted in pamphlets by the Whigs and helped to destroy Van Buren politically.

A song sung by the Whigs at campaign rallies and by the man on the street during the campaign of 1840 clearly shows how successful the Whigs were in projecting their distinct stereotyped images of the two candidates.

Old Tip he wears a homespun coat
He has no ruffled shirt-wirt-wirt
But Mart he has the golden plate
And he's a little squirt-wirt-wirt.

With scarcely a mention of any important issues, the Whigs triumphantly won the election. The log cabin campaign so deliberately and successfully launched to put Harrison into the White House was even more remarkable because the truth about Harrison was that he was actually a highly educated, cultured man. He was the son of a signer of the Declaration of Independence, lived on a two-thousand-acre estate, had no need to do physical farm labor and undoubtedly preferred the comforts of his pleasant home and his bourbon to a cabin and hard cider. As for his being a war hero, in the Battle of Tippecanoe Harrison lost more men than the Indians did and the battle itself was not considered decisive.

The aristocrat Stereotype that the Whigs presented of Martin Van Buren was equally false. Van Buren came from common stock, the son of a tavern-keeper, and although he was somewhat of a dandy about his appearance, he spent less money on the White House than any of his predecessors. Van Buren may, or may not, have been a better man for the job than Harrison. The point is that voters were offered Stereotypes—not actual men.

Although the log cabin Stereotype was important for a time, the war hero Stereotype in the long run has done more. It was certainly of immeasurable value in sweeping the following into office: George Washington, Andrew Jackson, William Henry Harrison, Zachary Taylor, Ulysses S. Grant, Theodore Roosevelt and Dwight D. Eisenhower. Seven Presidents out of thirty-two is not a bad average for the war hero Stereotype. (Other Presidents served in wars and were

GEN: ANDREW JACKSON.
THE HERO OF NEW·ORLEANS.
Lith. & Pub. by N.Currier 2 Spruce St N.Y.

A lithograph of Andrew Jackson in full military regalia. As the "Hero of New Orleans" in the War of 1812, Andrew Jackson was one of the first Presidents to use the image of the "War hero" (as well as his log-cabin background) to win the presidency in 1828. *The Harry T. Peters Collection, Museum of the City of New York*

HARRISONIAN

BALL ROLLING.

KEEP THE

WILLIAM HENRY HARRISON THE FARMER OF NORTH BEND.

RALLY!

A General Meeting

Will be held at the Old COURT ROOM, [Riey's building]

On Saturday Evening,

The 18th instant, at early candle light.   A punctual atten-
dance is requested.

MESSRS. DAVIS, BOTKIN, KEATING

And others, will address the Meeting.

July 17, 1840.

R. P. TODD, *Chairman*
Vigilance Committee.

A Harrison rally broadside using the Stereotype of the "log cabin" and showing presidential candidate Harrison, "the farmer of North Bend," hard at work plowing (with a barrel of hard cider comfortably close at hand!). Harrison actually lived in a 16-room house on a 2,000-acre estate near Cincinnati. *Library of Congress*

The cover of a piece of music written expressly for the Harrison 1840 presidential campaign—"General Harrison's Log Cabin March and Quick Step." *Library of Congress*

GENERAL HARRISON'S
LOG CABIN MARCH
A QUICK STEP

Published by SAM.L CARUSI Baltimore

GRANNY HARRISON DELIVERING THE COUNTRY OF THE *EXECUTIVE FEDERALIST.*

Printed & Pub. by H.R.Robinson, N.º 52 Courtland St. N.Y. & cor.º Avenue Washington D.C.

An early political cartoon during the Harrison–Van Buren campaign of 1840, which reflects the "image" the Harrison supporters wanted the people to believe about President Van Buren—that he was one of the hated aristocrats, trying to turn the White House into a royal palace. *Library of Congress*

This cartoon is from *Leslie's Illustrated Newspaper* in the 1850's. It carries the caption, "Unrestricted immigration and its results. A possible curiosity of the Twentieth Century. The last Yankee." The cartoon, one of many of its type, reflects the Fear Appeal propaganda of the "Know-Nothing" Party against the foreign immigrants destroying the "American way of life." *Library of Congress*

UNRESTRICTED IMMIGRATION AND ITS RESULTS.—A POSSIBLE CURIOSITY OF THE TWENTIETH CENTURY.
THE LAST YANKEE.
SEE PAGE 98.

Bring me before a Court
Maria Monk

Maria Monk's supposedly true autobiography of her cruel life in a convent, although later proved false, sold well and helped inflame the minds and emotions of American readers against all Roman Catholics, and further, through Misleading Association, against all foreign immigrants with "foreign" religious beliefs and ideas. *Rare Book Division, the New York Public Library, Astor, Lenox, and Tilden Foundations*

The "Know-Nothing" Party propaganda was used to incite fears that Roman Catholicism would control the nation, and through the schools, the nation's children. The same sort of Fear Appeal propaganda was used in the 1950's to suggest that communism was controlling the schools, and still later against racial minorities attending "white" schools. *Michael Choukas,* Propaganda Comes of Age (*Public Affairs Press*)

THE SHADOW IN OUR SCHOOLS.

NEW YORK CITY.—SCENE OF THE RIOT AT ELM PARK, EIGHTH AVENUE AND NINETIETH STREET, BETWEEN PROTESTANT AND CATHOLIC IRISH, ON TUESDAY, JULY 13, 1870.—See Page 316.

The racial and religious fears and hatreds aroused by the "Know-Nothing" Party against immigrants and Catholics did not end overnight. *Harpers Weekly* showed this scene of violence, which took place in New York City between Protestants and Catholics in July, 1870. Today, the same emotional appeals to fears and prejudice have brought about riots and violence between blacks and whites in our cities. *Harpers Weekly, July 12, 1870.*

Abraham Lincoln, even after he had achieved considerable success as a lawyer, was still portrayed in this campaign poster of 1858 as "Old Abe, the railsplitter," to remind voters of his log-cabin origin and to appeal to the vote of the "common man." *Courtesy Chicago Historical Society*

97

ROMISH POLITICS—ANY THING TO BEAT GRANT.

This cartoon, with ridicule, pictorial Name Calling, and Misleading Association, helped to defeat and destroy Horace Greeley, who ran against Grant for the presidency in 1872. Greeley is shown making a pact with an ape-like Irish Catholic in order to win votes, while a priest skulks in the background. The cartoonist, Thomas Nast (1840–1902) was one of America's most famous cartoonists. His pen helped elect Grant, Hayes, and Cleveland, and helped destroy New York City's graft-ridden political Tweed ring. *Harpers Weekly, August 17, 1872*

A Republican campaign poster of 1872, using the "just plain folks" Appeal to gain the vote of the working man. Ulysses Grant had been, of course, a general, and had hated the short time he worked in his father's tannery as a youth. The vice-presidential candidate was a Senator from Massachusetts who had made his fortune as a shoe manufacturer. *Library of Congress*

war heroes, but their campaigns were not based on this stereotype.)

Whether or not these seven men made good Presidents is not the question here. The question is: Why did the people vote for them? Because of the man's actual qualities and beliefs on national issues—or because of the Stereotype?

It is easy to see, logically, that the log cabin Stereotype can be misleading. The war hero Stereotype can be equally so. The qualities that make a man brave or successful in war do not necessarily make him wise enough to be a President in peacetime. President Grant's administration was riddled with scandals and corruption. President Taylor, another war hero, was one of our most ineffective Presidents. On the other hand, a man's coming from a log cabin or being a war hero does not prevent him—the man hidden behind the stereotype—from being a good President. But voters who voted for a Stereotype deserve no credit for the real man's policies and performance in office.

Yet, relatively speaking, the propaganda used in 1840 was harmless compared to the propaganda used in the congressional and state election campaigns of 1854 and 1855.

In these campaigns, the propaganda mounted by a new political party was not only dangerous but, if the party had gone on to win the Presidential election of 1856, could have undermined our free system of government. The political party was officially known as the American party, but it was better known as the Know-Nothing party. The nickname was taken from the fact that membership in the party was often secret, and when members were questioned, they would reply, "I know nothing about it." The platform of the Know-Nothing party, whose members called themselves the Nativists, was simple. They were anti-Catholic and anti-foreigner. Only native-born Protestant Americans, they believed, should have the right to vote and to hold public office.

The beliefs of the Know-Nothing party originated in the 1820's and 1830's, when a wave of anti-Catholic feeling swept from England to the United States. Since many of the Irish, Italian and German immigrants coming to America at that particular period were of the Roman Catholic faith, the feeling against Catholics was enlarged to include all incoming foreigners. This Misleading Association Device, as well as an Appeal to Fear, formed the basis for the Know-Nothing party's propaganda efforts. The "no popery" propaganda of the party was spread through cheaply produced pamphlets, tracts and books to almost every home in the country.

The writers used the propaganda devices of Name Calling without proof; Loaded Words; and Glittering Generalities. They also used Selection, presenting only "their" part of the truth; they over-simplified situations and problems, emphasizing only "their" answers; and, above all, they used Misleading Association. Their Appeals were to the fears, rather than the reason, of voters. Yet, to be fair, many of the writers of this propaganda literature, some of whom were Protestant churchmen, were sincerely afraid that the Catholics, swelling in numbers, not only planned to take over the country but quite literally move the Vatican to the Mississippi Valley of the United States!

The titles of these pamphlets and books—taking only a few out of the hundreds that were published—tell enough of the propaganda story:

> *The Papal Conspiracy Exposed*
> *Our Country Safe from Romanism*
> *Popery an Enemy to Civil and Religious Liberty*
> *and Dangerous to our Republic*
> *Rosamond; or, a Narrative of the Captivity and*
> *Sufferings of an American Female under the*
> *Popish Priests*

Open Convents or Nunneries and Popish Semi-
naries Dangerous to the Morals and Degrad-
ing to the Character of a Republican Country
The Escaped Nun; or, Disclosures of Convent Life
and the Confessions of a Sister of Charity
Imminent Dangers to the Free Institution of the
United States through Foreign Immigration
A Startling Disclosure of the Secret Workings of
the Jesuits
America and Americans Versus the Papacy and
the Catholics

The most sensational book, and the most popular, was entitled *Awful Disclosures of the Hotel Dieu Nunnery of Montreal,* written by Maria Monk and published in 1836. The story told of Maria's captivity as a young girl in a convent and the cruel and lascivious behavior of priests toward the nuns there. According to the book, Maria finally managed to escape and write her tale. The story was proven to be completely false, and Maria, a woman of dubious character, eventually died in prison. But the book became a sensational best-seller and convinced many non-Catholics that convents and monasteries should not be allowed in the United States.

The Nativists of the Know-Nothing party succeeded because the social conditions of the United States in the mid-nineteenth century made their over-stated propaganda believable. Foreigners were pouring into the country. Native-born citizens began to feel overwhelmed, outnumbered by people who spoke foreign tongues and still followed foreign ways. Also, a number of the immigrants wanted their children to attend Catholic and not public schools, and insisted in a dozen states that tax money be diverted to Catholic schools.

But the greatest fear of the members of the Know-Nothing

party was that the economy of the country was being ruined. Immigrants were willing to work for lower pay, taking away jobs from native born. Many immigrants had to be supported by hard-pressed public welfare. The Nativists could point to statistics that showed that 50 percent of the crimes in the country were being committed by immigrants. Also, sections of cities where immigrants lived tended to be or become slums and corrupt political machines like Tammany in New York bought immigrant votes at the polls.

Frightened by these disrupting, if temporary, circumstances, the Know-Nothing party circulated their propaganda through more than 125 religious magazines and newspapers, and hired roving orators to speak throughout the country against Catholicism and foreigners. Native-born citizens, most of them Protestant, read and listened and began to fear.

In the congressional elections of 1854, the Know-Nothing party scored astonishing victories. But, strangely enough, two years later, their Presidential candidate, Martin Fillmore, was defeated. He was defeated, in a way, because the Know-Nothing party propaganda was too successful. It concentrated on the human emotions of fear and hatred, calling for immediate action, and so inflamed the emotions of people against Catholics that bloody riots broke out in cities like Boston, St. Louis and New Haven.

Lives of priests and nuns were threatened, churches destroyed and convents burned. The rising bloodshed and mass hysteria made many citizens, who might otherwise have voted for the Know-Nothing party, step back appalled and begin to question the policies behind and the results of this fear propaganda.

Also, the American party had made at least two other mistakes: First, their members had been too secretive about their activities; many Americans were suspicious of secret organizations. Second, the Know-Nothing party's propaganda material was often so blown-up that it was easy for opponents to stick pins in it—and to make fun of it. Ridicule—humor that is used to cut things down to size—always has strong popular propaganda appeal. People do not like to be associated with objects of ridicule. Partly because of the shocking violence and partly because of the ridicule, Fillmore did go down in defeat—though not overwhelmingly.

What finally destroyed the Know-Nothing party and its fear-based propaganda was the ever-changing American scene and its ever-changing problems. A new crisis appeared in the 1850's—a real threat to the nation, greater than the apparent threat from foreign immigration. Southerners and Northerners within the Know-Nothing party began to split over this rising national issue: slavery. The quarrel over slavery eventually brought civil war, and an end to much of the influence of the Know-Nothing party.

The Know-Nothing party could have been a grave danger to American democracy, but not because the party used propaganda. All political parties and campaigns do that— for "good" and "bad" causes. The propaganda itself was only a force; the devices employed were old and common ones, still in use today. It was the goal of that propaganda—to build fear and division among Americans—that formed the danger.

Although the propaganda of the Know-Nothing party was widespread for its day, it could not compare in scope or intensity with the highly organized campaigns of modern-day political parties. It wasn't until 1896, in a remarkable Presidential election, that one man set a pattern for all future political campaigns to follow—as propaganda and politics moved into the twentieth century.

Political Propaganda Moves Into the Twentieth Century: Media and the Masses

THE ELECTION of 1896 was one of the closest fought in American history. The candidates were William McKinley, Republican, and William Jennings Bryan, Democrat. Any voter of that day would have said that the election was decided on the issue of "free silver." More probably, the election was decided by a triumph of new over old propaganda methods.

The United States in the 1890's was suffering from a serious financial depression. Faced with high interest rates and in desperate need of freer flow of money, the farmers, small merchants and workingmen favored free silver coinage. Releasing silver limitations would increase the amount of money in circulation. Bankers and big businessmen, on the other hand, were sure such a money policy would bring economic disaster, endangering the gold standard and the value of the dollar. So the battle line between the "haves" and the "have-nots" was drawn.

The Democrats favored free silver and the have-nots. At the Democratic convention, the name of young William Jennings Bryan was not one put in nomination. But, in one impassioned speech, the "boy orator" from Nebraska swept aside all other contenders. He believed in his cause, and he was superb—in the old style of political propaganda.

In his speech he Name-called the Eastern bankers the "financial harpies of Wall Street" and the "most merciless and unscrupulous gang of speculators on earth." With Loaded Words, he accused them of trying to "enslave" Western farmers and laboring men, who were then described by him with such Glittering Words as "chosen people," "embattled farmers" and "hardy pioneers."

The conclusion of Bryan's speech has gone down in history. It brought the convention crowd of 20,000 to their feet in wild applause:

> . . . *we will answer their demand for a gold standard by saying to them: You shall not press down upon the brow of labor this crown of thorns, you shall not crucify mankind upon a cross of gold.*

It was a strikingly effective use of Misleading Association —associating the laborers' and the Democratic party's cause with religion and Jesus. The Republicans, in this case, were doing the crucifying. The speech launched Bryan in a great wave of semi-religious, almost hysterical emotionalism, upon his campaign for the American Presidency.

In three months, he had traveled more than 18,000 miles and made six hundred political speeches, a remarkable record not surpassed to this day. Wherever he spoke, crowds responded enthusiastically to his emotion-charged appeals and chanted in response to his evangelistic fervor, "Bryan, Bryan! No crown of thorns, no cross of gold!"

Against Bryan and his silver-tongued oratory stood Mark Hanna, a Cleveland capitalist and chairman of the Republican National Committee, the man who masterminded McKinley's campaign. Hanna was the first modern-style propagandist. He introduced in this election of 1896 the beginnings of our present-day, computerized and efficiently organized Presidential campaigns. It was the first political campaign in which the propaganda was consolidated under one man (Hanna) and channeled through a central office down to state and local committees and ward-heelers. It was also the first time opinion polls were used to determine the feelings of voters. And, as a consequence, it was the most expensive political campaign to date.

Hanna not only used all possible communication media to distribute his propaganda, but he used his propaganda with great efficiency. By taking geographic polls throughout the country, he determined where support for McKinley was the weakest. When Iowa was discovered to be favoring Bryan, trainloads of pamphlets and dozens of speakers were rushed there immediately to turn voters toward McKinley, until the state was thought to be safely in the Republican camp.

Well aware that McKinley could not hope to compete with Bryan's oratory, Hanna sent 1,400 skilled speakers to all parts of the country to speak against Bryan and emphasize the evils of free-silver coinage.

With no popular Stereotype he could use—McKinley did not fit in with the log cabin man or the war hero—Hanna turned to building a "father" image. Like a good father, McKinley, a portly, stern-looking man, was pictured in his campaign posters promising his family—the voters —a "full dinner pail." Hanna risked no face-to-face, voice-to-voice comparisons with Bryan that might destroy this image. Instead he had McKinley conduct what was called a "front porch campaign."

McKinley never left his home in Canton, Ohio. Delegations of voters chosen from all walks of life were brought, their railway fares paid, to Canton. McKinley would welcome them on his front porch, deliver a prepared speech and give prepared answers to prepared questions—all with duly prepared publicity. McKinley's image, that of a calm, responsible fatherly man, staying sensibly at home, not rushing frantically around the country speaking a dozen times a day as Bryan was doing, was carefully projected to voters.

Of course, Hanna did not rely alone on the voters that were brought to Canton. He made sure that every voter in the country was approached. Thus, 120,000,000 copies of 275 different pamphlets, published in nine different languages, came like a paper landslide out of New York and Chicago. These pamphlets appealed to the economic fears of the workingman and small merchant, predicting the terrible fate that would befall the country if Bryan were elected (and free silver succeeded). Factories would cut production; railroads would reduce the number of trains running; the value of people's savings would be cut in half and jobs would disappear.

Apart from his fear appeals, Hanna used other tried and historically effective propaganda devices. Newspapers, for example, were fed a steady stream of columns and cartoons Name calling Bryan as an "anarchist," a "slobbering demagogue" and a "paranoiac" bent on destroying the country.

And if Bryan could use the propaganda device of misleading Association, so could Hanna. Bryan's Cross of Gold speech had associated free coinage of silver with religion.

The Republican workers for McKinley turned to the equally misleading association of sound gold-standard currency with patriotism—in the symbol of the American flag.

Even McKinley, figuratively wrapping himself in the American flag, proclaimed in one of his front porch speeches: "I am glad to know that the people in every part of the country mean to be devoted to one flag, and that the glorious Stars and Stripes; that the people of the country this year mean to maintain the financial honor of the country as sacredly as they maintain the honor of the flag."

McKinley workers passed out campaign buttons that bore only a picture of the American flag. All over the country Hanna organized flag parades for McKinley, a solid stream of marchers, each waving the American flag. Watching Hanna's strategy, Theodore Roosevelt, later to become President of the United States himself, was moved to complain that Hanna was selling McKinley "like a patent medicine."

Because this new style of propaganda campaigning was so much more expensive than the old, Hanna added one more modern touch: he deliberately assessed campaign funds from big businesses and wealthy men, like the Standard Oil Company and J. P. Morgan. Historians conservatively estimate Hanna spent at least $4,000,000 against Bryan's $300,000—and a dollar went much further in those days!

Whatever the final costs, the election returns were as follows: McKinley, 7,035,638; Bryan, 6,467,946.

It is doubtful if many voters ever understood the free-silver issue or the complex economic problems facing the United States in 1896. Even today, no one can say with certainty whether Bryan or McKinley was the best man for the job. One can say that each candidate believed in his cause, and each candidate chose the kind of campaign that he thought would win.

Both used the common propaganda devices and appeals, and, of the two candidates, it can be said that Bryan, personally, seemed more skillful in their use. But he made the mistake of relying on one old-fashioned medium—his oratory. He was defeated by a new-style Presidential campaign that used every possible communication medium, a widely spread variety of propaganda devices, including the important strategy of repetition—and a great deal of money.

In today's modern political campaigns, organized, analyzed and plotted down to the last detail, the propaganda devices have not essentially changed. In the nineteenth century, Andrew Jackson was Name-called a "home wrecker, gambler and murderer," and Thomas Jefferson, "Mad Tom"; in the twentieth century, Franklin D. Roosevelt was called "Mother Goosevelt," and President Nixon, "tricky Dicky." Similarly, the use of political cartoons to Name-call and ridicule a candidate have not changed much.

Remember the Know-Nothing party and its Appeals to fear of Catholic power in the 1850's? The same Fear Appeal was used against Catholic Al Smith in 1928, and in 1960 against John Kennedy. Rumors were spread that Rome would be the capital of the United States if Kennedy won.

And remember the Know-Nothing party's Appeals to Fear that foreign newcomers were lowering educational standards, and increasing crime and slums and welfare payments? The same Fear Appeals were raised by the American party in 1968, with George Wallace as its candidate, this time not against foreigners but against the black people in American society.

Another basis of many early, successful Presidential campaigns was the Stereotype war hero. This Stereotype was also the basis of the twentieth-century campaigns of Theodore Roosevelt and Dwight D. Eisenhower. Roosevelt, in his campaign for governor of New York State, even had seven uniformed Rough Riders travel with him. At each campaign stop, just before Roosevelt began his speech, a Rough Rider would blow a charge on a cavalry bugle. Although leading the Rough Rider charge up San Juan Hill in the Spanish American War of 1898 was to Roosevelt's credit, his brave dash did not, really, qualify him for governor—or for President. Roosevelt did become a popular President. So did Eisenhower, whose campaign dealt little with current issues, except references to ending the war in Korea. He won the Presidency as a war hero of World War II.

The Selection Device of the Scapegoat in political campaigns has continued to be much in use. In the McKinley-Bryan campaign, McKinley supporters blamed the "anarchists" (people who favor political disorder and violence as opposed to formal government) for the economic danger to the country. Bryan's supporters blamed the Wall Street "tyrants." Each side chose a scapegoat for all that was wrong with the country. Today, ultra-conservative Republican candidates blame Communists for the country's troubles, while ultra-liberal Democrats blame "the Establishment" for holding up the country's progress. Scapegoats are easy answers to problems that are complicated. Throughout history, men have chosen and are given scapegoats— in order to avoid sharing any of the blame themselves. By making someone else guilty, we become innocent. Also, simple solutions save the voters the trouble and effort of thinking for themselves.

Over-simplification of political slogans has not changed a good deal either. In 1920, the Republican candidate Warren Harding successfully employed the slogan "Return to Normal Law and Order" to win votes. In 1968, the Republican candidate Richard Nixon just as successfully used the slogan "Law and Order." Propaganda slogans do not have to change. They are meant to "sound" good, and to

The whirlwind old-style campaign of William Jennings Bryan, presidential candidate of 1896 for the Democrats against McKinley, was undoubtedly as effective as the tireless candidate could make it. Bryan, shown here in one of his famous oratorical poses, was considered one of the finest speakers of his day. *Brown Brothers*

William McKinley's campaign against William Jennings Bryan in 1896 for the presidency was called the "front porch" campaign—because that was where, for the most part, McKinley stayed. But his campaign, masterminded by Mark Hanna, Chairman of the Republican Party, was broadly based, using the modern style of political propaganda. *Harpers Weekly, Aug. 29, 1896*

As opposed to Bryan's youth (he was only 36 when he first ran for President against McKinley), McKinley projected in his campaign of 1896 the image of a calm figure of fatherly responsibility, "Our home defender." *Library of Congress*

THE SACRILEGIOUS CANDIDATE.

No man who drags into the dust the most sacred symbols of the Christian world is fit to be president of the United States.

To combat the semi-religious fervor aroused in voters by Bryan's Cross of Gold speech, Bryan was Name-called by his opponents, "The Sacrilegious Candidate." The caption on this *Judge* magazine reads, "No man who drags into the dust the most sacred symbols of the Christian world is fit to be President of the United States." Often, as propaganda, symbols can be more effective than words. *Judge magazine, September, 1896*

When William McKinley ran again for President in 1900 (this time with Theodore Roosevelt as his running mate) once more he was the fatherly image promising the voters "four years more of the full dinner pail." The full dinner pail with its Appeal of financial security became a popular symbol for McKinley, much as the Cross of Gold had for Bryan. *Library of Congress*

WILLIAM McKINLEY   THEODORE ROOSEVELT

FOUR YEARS MORE OF THE FULL DINNER PAIL

In this campaign poster of 1900 is repeated the Misleading Association slogan Bryan made famous in his 1896 speech, "No crown of thorns, no cross of gold." Note also the use of such Glittering Generalities as Liberty, Justice, and Humanity as "The Issue—1900." *Library of Congress*

Indirect Name Calling and Misleading Association used against John F. Kennedy as Democratic presidential candidate in the 1960 campaign. In the 1928 campaign, Roman Catholic presidential candidate Al Smith was also pictured kneeling to the Pope. *Fair Campaign Practices Committee*

This 1935 cartoon titled "Grassroots Convention" views politicians' use of the vote-getting Stereotype, the "ready-made" image of Lincoln. A Lincoln-type would appear to be a man of the people, poor, honest, compassionate, courageous. A Democratic presidential aspirant of the 1972 campaign, Senator Muskie, has been referred to as a "Lincoln type." But then, Lincoln himself also used a Stereotype to win office amid the politics of his day—that of the rail-splitting, log-cabin man. *Fitzpatrick*, St. Louis Post Dispatch

If these two men were running for President today, which candidate do you think would project the better "image" on television? Abraham Lincoln with his bearded, brooding face and falsetto voice, or the silver-haired Warren G. Harding with the squared jaw and straightforward gaze? *Library of Congress*

(RIGHT , TOP) A political ad that appeared in many newspapers during the presidential campaign of 1928. The Appeal is obvious—financial security, "a chicken for every pot," much like McKinley's "full dinner pail." Promises made in propaganda appeals, however, cannot always be delivered. Herbert Hoover was overwhelmingly elected President in 1928, but in 1929 the country began the worse depression in its history. *St. Louis Public Library, St. Louis, Mo.*

(RIGHT, BOTTOM) In the Kennedy–Nixon presidential race of 1960, Democratic Kennedy's wealth was used against him. Republican Lincoln was associated with Republican Nixon. *Fair Campaign Practices Committee*

A Chicken *for* Every Pot

THE Republican Party isn't a *"Poor Man's Party."* Republican prosperity has erased that degrading phrase from our political vocabulary.

The Republican Party is *equality's* party—*opportunity's* party—*democracy's* party, the party of *national* development, not *sectional* interests—the *impartial* servant of every State and condition in the Union.

Under higher tariff and lower taxation, America has stabilized output, employment and dividend rates.

Republican efficiency has filled the workingman's dinner pail—and his gasoline tank *besides*—made telephone, radio and sanitary plumbing *standard* household equipment. And placed the whole nation in the *silk stocking class.*

During eight years of Republican management, we have built more and better homes, erected more skyscrapers, passed more benefactory laws, and more laws to regulate and purify immigration, inaugurated more conservation measures, more measures to standardize and increase production, expand export markets, and reduce industrial and human junk piles, than in any previous quarter century.

Republican prosperity is written on *fuller* wage envelops, written in factory chimney smoke, written on the walls of new construction, written in savings bank books, written in mercantile balances, and written in the peak value of stocks and bonds.

Republican prosperity has *reduced* hours and *increased* earning capacity, silenced *discontent*, put the proverbial "chicken in every pot." And a car in every backyard, to boot.

It has *raised* living standards and *lowered* living costs.

It has restored financial confidence and enthusiasm, changed *credit* from a rich man's privilege to a *common* utility, *generalized* the use of time-saving devices and released women from the thrall of *domestic drudgery.*

It has provided every county in the country with its concrete road and knitted the highways of the nation into a *unified* traffic system.

Thanks to Republican administration, farmer, dairyman and merchant can make deliveries in *less* time and at *less* expense, can borrow *cheap* money to re-fund exorbitant mortgages, and stock their pastures, ranges and shelves.

Democratic management *impoverished* and *demoralized* the railroads, led packing plants and tire factories into *receivership*, squandered billions on *impractical* programs.

Democratic mal-administration issued *further* billions on mere "scraps of paper," then encouraged foreign debtors to believe that their loans would never be called, and bequeathed to the Republican Party the job of *mopping up the mess.*

Republican administration has *restored* to the railroads solvency, efficiency and par securities.

It has brought the rubber trades through panic and chaos, brought down the prices of crude rubber by smashing *monopolistic rings*, put the tanner's books in the *black* and secured from the European powers formal acknowledgment of their obligations.

The Republican Party rests its case on a record of stewardship and performance.

Its Presidential and Congressional candidates stand for election on a platform of sound practice, Federal vigilance, high tariff, Constitutional integrity, the conservation of natural resources, *honest* and *constructive* measures for agricultural relief, sincere enforcement of the laws, and the right of *all* citizens, regardless of *faith* or *origin*, to share the benefits of opportunity and justice.

Wages, dividends, progress and prosperity say,

"Vote *for* Hoover"

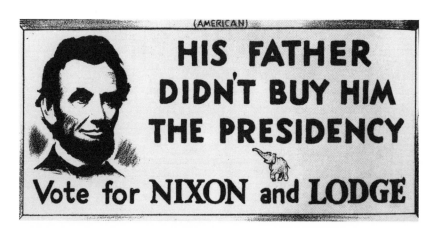

(AMERICAN)

HIS FATHER DIDN'T BUY HIM THE PRESIDENCY

Vote for NIXON and LODGE

This political advertisement favoring Democrat Lyndon Johnson in his 1964 presidential campaign against Republican Barry Goldwater was intended to show that the danger of atomic war was greater if Johnson did not win. This Fear Appeal, as used on television, "came alive" with a real child picking daisies and counting, ending with an actual explosion after count-down. *Michael Choukas,* Propaganda Comes of Age (*Public Affairs Press*)

This propagandistic material, used in the Johnson–Goldwater campaign of 1964, Name-calls the Democratic party (and Democratic Presidents) warmongers. The Misleading Association is that the Republican Party is the party of peace. As propaganda study, it is interesting to note that two of the Republican Presidents cited—Theodore Roosevelt and Dwight D. Eisenhower—essentially won the presidency through "war hero" Stereotypes. *Michael Choukas,* Propaganda Comes of Age (*Public Affairs Press*)

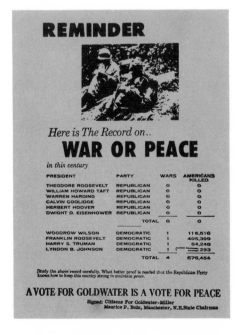

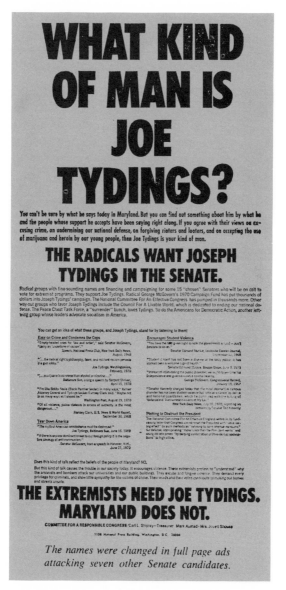

The names were changed in full page ads attacking seven other Senate candidates.

This full-page advertisement was used in the 1970 congressional elections to attack Tydings and seven other senatorial candidates, including Muskie of Maine, Stevenson of Illinois, and Tunney of California. The advertisement accused the candidates of "excusing crime," "undermining our national defense," "forgiving rioters and looters," and "accepting the use of marijuana and heroin by our young people." By Misleading Association, any voter for Tydings (or whatever other candidate was named) favored radicals and extremists. The paid advertisement reportedly appeared in 61 newspapers, but some newspapers refused to handle it. *Samuel J. Archibald, ed.*, The Pollution of Politics (*Public Affairs Press*) mean little or nothing. Here are some other twentieth-century campaign slogans.

The New Deal   (*For whom?*)
Franklin Roosevelt

The New Frontier   (*For whom and precisely what is a frontier?*)
John Kennedy

All the Way with LBJ   (*All the way where?*)
Lyndon B. Johnson

In your heart, you know he's right.   (*And in your head?*)
Barry Goldwater

Though the propaganda devices found in political campaigns have not changed much over the years, some of them have come up with new twists because of the new communications media available. Slogans, for example, are now dinned into voters' ears over and over again by radio and television, even sung in jingles, to be remembered almost unconsciously like commercials. Motion pictures and television have also created new "images" to be used by candidates, images that take the place of actual individual attributes or lack of them.

A few candidates have been able to utilize this film "image" in an indirect way. The successes of former actor George Murphy in his election to the Senate and former actor Ronald Reagan in his election to the governorship of California must be credited partly to their previous public exposure as "good guys" in dozens of Hollywood films. They had "good images" before their campaigns had even begun.

Most candidates are not that lucky, of course. They may appear on television in millions of American living rooms, and the image each creates can be the deciding factor in his winning or losing. Yet that image may rest on something as superficial as a good microphone voice and the right make-up. Many supporters of Richard Nixon still insist that it was his dark-jowled, swarthy appearance on the television screen (his make-up artist was blamed) during the television debates with John F. Kennedy that lost Nixon that particular election.

To put the situation historically, if Abraham Lincoln were to campaign on television, his brooding, craggy features, beard and falsetto voice might prevent his election. On the other hand, Warren Harding, handsome and wise-looking, appeared every inch a President. He had what might be called "instant image." Historians regard him as one of our worse Presidents.

Present-day political campaigns must make use of all communication media available—and these campaigns must be nation-wide. Hanna only began the modern approach. Today, Presidential candidates employ public relations agencies to make certain the best possible national campaign is used and the best possible Presidential image is presented to the voters. Since political propaganda over the new mass media—television, films, radio—is very complicated, public-relations firms are often hired by today's political candidates —specialists who understand the techniques involved in working with the new media.

Television has had other effects on political propaganda. Because of the television cost and time limitations, political "commercials" must be kept short, forcing an over-simplification of many points. Although cartoons and slogans in print and even stereotypes present an over-simplified version of a candidate, the emotional impact of a television presentation on the voter is much greater. The propaganda devices have not changed, but they are much more effective.

Television engages both sight and hearing, and even affects the muscular tension of the viewer. Television may suggest added appeals to taste and to smell, and the "story" given in motion comes alive.

The following two political campaign television commercials will give some idea of why propaganda has become more effective. In 1964, when incumbent Democratic President Lyndon Johnson campaigned against Republican Barry Goldwater, the Democratic party ran a one-minute television commercial, showing a pretty child in a peaceful meadow picking petals from a daisy and counting off the petals as she did so. Suddenly, however, the childish counting became the countdown for an atomic bomb explosion. As the terrifying mushroom cloud filled the sky, a stern voice warned, "Vote for President Johnson on November 3. The stakes are too high for you to stay home." The age-old Appeal to Fear was the threat of atomic warfare destroying children; the Misleading Association was that a vote for Goldwater automatically meant a vote for such a war.

The Republicans, too, have used this strong Fear Appeal in their television commercials. In 1968 when Richard Nixon ran against Hubert Humphrey, a Republican party commercial showed the face of Humphrey, smiling and laughing, superimposed over scenes of riot, warfare, death and poverty. No spoken comment was necessary. The Misleading Association was that a vote for Humphrey meant a vote for a candidate so callous that he habitually laughed at or ignored these troubles.

Because of opposition party protests, both of these commercials were finally taken off television. But their impact had already been made.

A new twist has also been used in working with Hanna's opinion polls. Hanna used them as a means of finding out where more propaganda was needed to convince voters. In recent elections, the opinion polls themselves have been made a part of the propaganda Appeal. Thus, when a poll is taken of 500 people throughout the country, and it is found, to the satisfaction of those paying for the poll, that Jim Jones is the choice of the 500, then Bandwagon Appeal publicity is sent out: "Jim Jones is top choice—80 percent of the people polled prefer him." Most people are drawn to a winner.

In 1896, the Republican party spent $4 million to elect William McKinley to the Presidency. In 1968 the Republican party spent $29 million to bring in another winning candidate, Richard Nixon, with $12.6 million of that sum spent on radio and television broadcasts. Costs of political campaigning at all levels, not just for the Presidency, have risen from an estimated $140 million in 1952 to $300 million in 1968. The greatest rise was in the cost of radio and television broadcasts, which went from $6.1 million in 1952 to $56 million in 1968.

Propaganda, in itself, is not bad. It is a force that can be used for good, bad or neutral causes. So what is wrong with spending a lot of money on political campaigns and propaganda? There are at least two dangers. One is that the candidate may be "indebted" to those who furnish him with these large sums and may have to, in some political way, "pay back." The second danger is that there may be an overuse of the propaganda device of False Emphasis—too much newspaper space or too much radio-television time given to one candidate. This can mean that a wealthier candidate, supported by big-money interests, can outbuy and smother with propaganda any opposition. In Presidential campaigns, with two or even three big parties, all well supported, this has not yet happened.

What has happened, however, is that any minor party or independent candidate finds it a difficult, if not impossible, task to reach the eye and ear of the average voter. Should all minor party and independent candidates then be eliminated from our government? Or should all political parties, as in Great Britain, be limited by law in the time and money they can spend on any given campaign? Or should political campaigns be publicly, not privately, funded as they are in West Germany?

The problem has not been resolved in the United States. But in February, 1972, President Nixon signed a federal-election-spending bill designed to plug finance-reporting loopholes and to curb rising campaign costs. Certain limitations were placed on presidential and congressional candidates' spending on advertising—television, radio, newspapers, magazines, and outdoor display. However, no overall limit was imposed on total campaign spending, and the new law is considered difficult to enforce.

However, political propaganda—like all other forms of propaganda—does not succeed by expensive campaigns alone. Propaganda may fail because the audience does not respond to the Appeals offered. It may also fail because of too much spending. Political campaigns that incessantly flood the airways for months before an election may, in fact, widen "the credulity gap" of some voters. Well aware that they are being exposed to propaganda, but not educated to spot the common propaganda devices used, these voters become skeptical of anything said in political campaigns. They may refuse to vote at all.

Even in our sophisticated times, however, a voter of average intelligence—with some preparation and with a sense of humor—can learn to recognize Name Calling; can question the easy, meaningless Slogans; can note the Over-simplification of difficult problems and the use of Misleading Associations. He can look beyond the Appeals offered and discover what political "article" is actually being sold. He can refuse to accept Emotional Appeals and insist on reasonable discussion of issues. In fact, when a campaign offers no balanced discussion and makes only Emotional Appeals to fear, hatred or patriotism, any voter can draw his own logical conclusion about that candidate.

Propaganda has exerted great influence on our political history. But political campaigns occur only occasionally. As we shall see, propaganda has exerted an even greater and more surprising influence on our economic history. And economic propaganda affects us—all of us—every day.

Economic Propaganda: From Selling America to Selling Americans

". . . AIRE AND CLYMATE most sweete and wholesome . . . mountains making a sensible proffer of hidden treasure. . . . Indians . . . generally very loving and gentle, and doe entertaine and relieve our people with great kindnesse. . . ."

Words from an Emigration tract distributed by the chartered corporation, the Virginia Company in London.

At the time these words were advertising "Nova Brittania," settlers in that colony (Jamestown, Virginia) were so starved they were eating carcasses of dead comrades, had found not a molehill of hidden treasure, and were being killed off by the "gentle and loving" Indians. The first use of propaganda devices in the advertising of America was not to sell a product but to sell the country itself.

In the England of the seventeenth and eighteenth centuries, luxury products were already being advertised. The famous eighteenth-century English author Dr. Samuel Johnson referred to the "very numerous" London advertisements of perfumes, wigs, books, coffee, tea, spices and silk. Such advertisements usually stated only the goods and their prices, and did not utilize propaganda devices. But the great colonizers of those centuries did not find the selling of new continents so easy. Colonizers had to use propaganda appeals: treasure, romantic adventure, glory, even patriotism, conquest, "free" land. And they did not plainly give the price: disease, poor food or no food at all, hostile Indians, backbreaking labor, long freezing winters, dangerous sea travel, loneliness and very possibly death.

Nevertheless, people of the seventeenth and eighteenth centuries responded to the appeals, and so did people of the nineteenth century. From England, Sweden, Finland, Norway, Switzerland, Ireland and Germany they came, leaving loved ones and the safety of their homes to seek out a land where the streets were "paved with gold" and land was virtually free—according to the advertisements of steamship and railroad lines. The railroad and steamship advertisements, like those of early colonizers, did not mention price: city slums, sweat shops, travel in ship steerage, back-breaking labor, disease, loneliness. Such propaganda to promote emigration formed an important and necessary force in the building of the United States.

Outside of emigration tracts, however, propaganda was used very little in the printed advertising of the early days of the United States. In fact, in colonial days there was little printed advertising of any kind. Benjamin Franklin was among the first in the American colonies to place advertisements in his newspaper, the *Pennsylvania Gazette*. His, as well as other newspaper advertising, must have enjoyed some success because one of the protested taxes along with the tea and stamp tax, was a tax on colonial newspaper advertising.

As the young United States grew, industries grew and competition increased. So advertising increased. Producers of hand-operated washing machines, stoves and wagons, for example, wanted to reach a wider range of customers and create more customers.

Perhaps the most flamboyant users of early American economic propaganda were the patent-medicine sellers. In addition to their brightly painted wagons and musical entertainment to attract crowds, the patent-medicine men used the old traditional propaganda Appeals: Testimonial Appeals from a bearded Dr. Ezekiel Jones or a Reverend Isaiah Adams, or Just-plain-folks Appeals from Farmer Smith or Farmer Jones in the next county who is "just a plain fellow like you and swears by this medicine."

More professional and sometimes more subtle practitioners entered the economic propaganda field in the 1840's and 1850's. Volney Palmer in 1841 advertised himself as "Agent for Country Newspapers." His success made clear the usefulness of expanding advertising beyond local areas and coordinating a program of advertising; in short, with Volney Palmer the advertising agency was born. The methods that came into use then have not changed much since.

About that time, Sarah Hale, one of the most effective magazine editors of the day, in her Godey's Lady's Book (circulation 63,000 by 1851), presented high-fashion gowns displayed to best advantage on attractive models in high social-status surroundings, often accompanied by Loaded and Glittering Words. Buying the latest fashion to be with the 'in" crowd then, as now, was very much a part of fashion propaganda.

The title page of an emigration tract by Robert Johnson, 1609, advertising the Virginia Colony. *Rare Book Division, New York Public Library*

NOVA BRITANNIA.

OFFERING MOST

Excellent fruites by Planting in
VIRGINIA.

Exciting all such as be well affected
to further the same.

LONDON
Printed for SAMVEL MACHAM, and are to be sold at
his Shop in Pauls Church-yard, at the
Signe of the Bul-head.
1609.

Propaganda Appeals had to be strong to pull people from their families and homes in Europe to seek out an uncertain future in an almost unknown land. This print, "Departure from Home," in *Harpers Weekly*, June 24, 1858, shows a typical immigrant leave–taking for the United States. *Harpers Weekly, June 24, 1858*

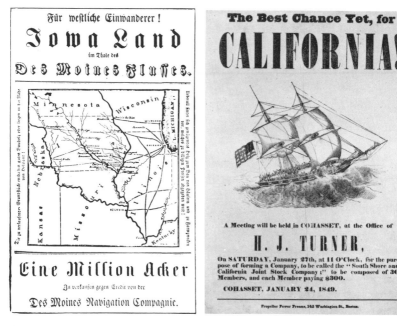

(ABOVE, LEFT) A poster distributed in Germany in the mid-nineteenth century, advertising a "million acres of Iowa land available to immigrants on easy credit from the Des Moines Navigation Company . . . with plenty of timber available for home and farm buildings." What the poster didn't mention were the blistering summers and freezing winters and the fact that, rather than owning wooden homes, most immigrants lived in sod houses on the open prairie. *Culver Pictures*

(BELOW) Early printers used the same type designs, such as this elephant, for a variety of advertisements. Canal and stage lines, river boats and railroads found advertising paid, and if the type design used was often the same, so were the propaganda Appeals. *Hornung,* Handbook of Early Advertising Art (*Dover*)

(ABOVE, RIGHT) Emigration tract—for the '49 Gold Rush to California. *Bostonian Society Library, Boston, Mass.*

Advertisements like this one appeared in western Europe and in eastern United States, "selling" America to prospective immigrants from Europe and to land-hungry easterners. *Harpers Weekly, June 15, 1876*

KANSAS PACIFIC RAILWAY LANDS - ASTONISH THE WORLD IN PRODUCTS OF WHEAT. FARMING MADE EASY AND PROFITS IMMENSE. 5,000,000 ACRES FOR SALE. VERY LOW PRICES. CREDIT LONG. SEND FOR COPY OF The Kansas Pacific Homestead, address S. J. Gilmore, Land Commissioner, Lawrence, Kansas.

Advertisement for Dakota lands in the United States which appeared in Great Britain in 1888, contrasting the happy New World with the sad Old World. Note bottom left picture and sign, "To America, Land of Free Homes," with various royalty and heads of states rushing to emigrate. *Library of Congress*

With the increase of manufacturing following the Civil War, the promotion afforded by advertising became indispensable for a growing economy. Cooking stoves, pianos, organs, and hand-operated washing machines were prominent in the biggest advertisements in newspapers and periodicals. This 1876 advertisement in *Harpers Weekly,* though mild in tone, uses Glittering Generalities of "best," "all modern improvements" and "many new and valuable inventions," along with the term "Uncle Sam Range." *Harpers Weekly, July 8, 1876*

The patent medicine advertisement—its Appeal that it will cure anything and everything! Often, as above, it was tied in with a Testimonial Appeal from an Indian medicine man. *Library of Congress*

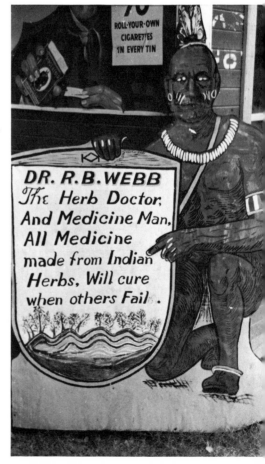

This patent medicine advertisement in an 1898 *Harpers Weekly,* apart from other Appeals and Glittering Generalities, offers a wide-sweeping Testimonial Appeal from Presidents to royalty. *Harpers Weekly, December 17, 1898*

Godey's Lady's Book, popular magazine of the 1850's and 1860's, pictured in color new dress fashions as they appeared—if your gown wasn't in *Godey's,* it wasn't in style! Then, as now, fashion relied on the Bandwagon Appeal, as well as the Romance Appeal. The editor of *Godey's,* Sarah Josepha Hale, not only set the pattern for future women's periodicals but was an early campaigner for women's rights, including the right of anesthesia in childbirth. *Godey's Lady's Book, June, 1850*

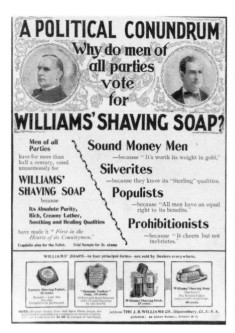

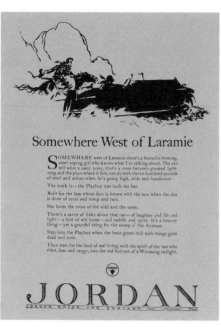

(ABOVE, LEFT) With the advent of new-style political techniques in the McKinley-Bryan presidential campaign in 1896, advertisers also began to turn toward modern methods. Although this advertisement has a slight Bandwagon Appeal, it is mostly geared to the contemporary event of the election and to the use of the Appeal to Humor of play on words and conundrum. *Judge magazine, 1896*

In the early 1900's, cars no longer needed to be hand-cranked. Women became automobile buyers. Jordan Motor Car Company declared its new model was built for "that broncho busting, steer roping girl somewhere west of Laramie." The romantic, adventurous woman Appeal appeared again in the 1960's when a similar girl of the West was pictured, along with a highly effective modern slogan, "Join the Dodge Rebellion." *Julian Watkins,* The 100 Greatest Advertisements (*Dover*)

Use of the American Presidents' "testimonials"—without their permission—gave authority and glamor Appeal to advertisements in the magazines of the early 1900's. *Life magazine, 1910*

There were dozens of automobile manufacturers in the United States in the early 1900's. To overcome the competition, the automobile industry began advertising. This Packard advertisement in *Life* magazine of July, 1910, used a slogan that was so good it was reused by other automobile advertisers over the years. *Life magazine, July, 1910*

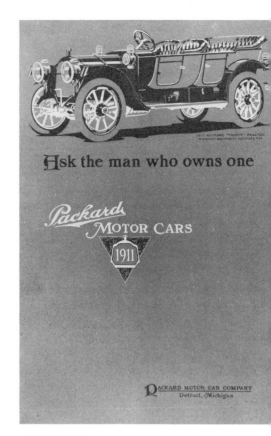

Automobile manufacturers by 1910 were aware buyers would not respond to mechanical details about the quality of a car. An Appeal found effective, yesterday and today, was Status. This advertisement for Pierce-Arrow appeared in *Life* magazine, September 1, 1910. *Life magazine, September 1, 1910*

In 1911, in the *Ladies Home Journal*, the slogan "A Skin You Love to Touch" was originated by Woodbury's. Its approach was much-copied down through the years. The Romantic and Sex Appeals, in the picture and slogan, were augmented in the Status Appeal at lower right of "She's another Woodbury Deb."

But recalling the use of Presidents in former advertisements, take note of the change to movie stars for Celebrity–Authority Appeal. For those who are not film-history buffs, Harold Lloyd, featured at top right, was an early Hollywood star. *Julian Watkins,* The 100 Greatest Advertisements (*Dover*)

137

WORLD'S HIGHEST STANDARD OF LIVING

In the 1930's, when the American economy was at its lowest ebb, America was still being "sold"—this time, to lift the morale of the people. However, normally effective and even truthful propaganda will not "work" if the environment and circumstances are strongly negative. *Library of Congress*

The Cadillac advertisement refers to the car's undoubtedly fine mechanical qualities, but only in small print. Most buyers would not understand the mechanical details anyway. What all do understand is the human desire to believe, "It speaks eloquently about you, yet barely whispers," and "Wherever Cadillac goes it makes complimentary remarks about its owner." Automobile manufacturers, over the decades, have learned their advertising must be based on Appeals to universal human desires or needs. *Courtesy of Cadillac Automobile Division*

HOTEL ST. REGIS

It speaks eloquently about you, yet barely whispers.

A modern advertiser turns to Youth Appeal, with a touch of light humor. Note that the product undoubtedly does bring quick, fresh energy, but the advertiser was aware such a statement was not enough. The picture carries a further message, of course, as do the words "flip" and "zzzip"—youthful words. *Courtesy of Royal Crown Cola Co.*

Film personalities James Mason and Louis Jourdan are simply shown enjoying the Coronet ice cream—but it is an effective advertisement, with Authority–Celebrity Appeal. *Courtesy, H. P. Hood & Sons, Boston*

A modern advertisement with a touch of humor. And the Appeal is. . . .
Courtesy Bristol–Myers Products

Discover Tropical Mist...

FROM *Betty Crocker*

Perhaps the most provocative
new cake flavor in years.
A soft, citrus flavor. Delicate
as a jungle flower . . . refreshing
as a sudden waterfall.
Exotically different. So different,
Betty Crocker offers it in two mixes.
Tropical Mist Angel Food and
Tropical Mist Layer Cake.
Be adventurous. Discover both.
New Tropical Mist Cake Mixes.
only from Betty Crocker.

Two modern advertisements
which appeal by a stimulating
"taste"—through the eyes. Supported by tropical scenes, the
cake advertisement offers "soft
citrus flavor. Delicate as a jungle
flower . . . refreshing as a sudden waterfall." The soup advertisement sets up a humorous
association by the plays-on-
words of "on the Rocks,"
"straight," "cool," "habit-forming." Equally modern in this advertisement are the references to
nutritional needs and low cal-
ories.

*Used with permission
of General Mills, Inc.*

Soup on the Rocks!

*Campbell's is
the trademark of
the Campbell Soup
Company*

Wait, don't go away! This you're
going to like. Take a roomy glass
—short or tall. Fill it up with ice
cubes. Pour Campbell's Beef Broth
on the ice cubes, just as it comes
from the can. That's Soup on the
Rocks—and you'll enjoy it!

Take it straight—or experiment
a bit. Add a dash of Worcester-
shire, a bit of lemon (peel or juice).
Not that you have to—Campbell's
Beef Broth on the rocks doesn't
need any doctoring.

Habit-forming? Sure it is. Such a

pleasant habit—such a healthy
habit. Cool, cool Soup on the
Rocks. Refreshing! Satisfying! You'll
like it before meals, between meals
—when you get home from work.
Have Soup on the Rocks whenever you need a quick low-calorie
pickup. And serve it to the children
any time—it's pleasantly inexpensive. But don't let us keep you—is
there a can of Campbell's Beef

Broth in the house? Break out the
ice cubes—have Soup on the Rocks
—right now!

SOUPS SUPPLY BASIC
NUTRITIONAL NEEDS.

VITAMINS, MINERALS and LIQUIDS
—for general well being
PROTEINS—for upkeep and growth
CARBOHYDRATES—for energy

Once a day...<u>every</u> day...SOUP!

141

By the late nineteenth century, admen were going beyond the patent-medicine men's doctor-minister-farmer Testimonial Appeals, and using top men to sell their products: Presidents of the United States. George Washington, Ulysses S. Grant, Martin Van Buren and William McKinley were among the Presidents sharing this dubious distinction. Thomas Jefferson's name was used as a trademark for a rye whisky, and his home, Monticello, was falsely pictured beside a whisky still. Today, instead of Presidents, entertainers and sports celebrities are frequently used (but with permission and handsome payments).

One of the most unchanging in its use of propaganda devices has been the American automobile industry. In the early days, the automobile was pictured and its attributes given, if given at all, in glittering generalities. Today, we still see Glittering Word slogans: "Ford has a better idea!" "Strike a blow for originality!" "Take the Mustang pledge." "Get in with the in Crowd in a GS-400" (a 1967 Buick). "Escape from the ordinary in Olds Tornado." The automobile, in early days as now, was tied to universal human needs or desires—an Appeal to Sex, Status, Social Acceptance. Thus, the automobile was and often still is shown with a background of a beautiful woman and a palatial mansion —sex and status appeals.

The Playboy automobile of the early 1920's, made by Jordan Motor Corporation, was advertised as being for the "broncho busting, steer-roping girl"; modern-day Dodge advertisements have shown a picture of a pretty girl in Western clothes with the message "Join the Dodge Rebellion." The old Apperson car was pictured in front of the Taj Mahal or the Parthenon to show its association with culture and prestige; many modern-day cars are pictured in front of mansions or country clubs.

What does a palatial mansion, a pretty girl in Western

clothes, a handsome sportsman in front of a country club, have to do with the value of a car? Nothing. But the automobile industry, turning out thousands of cars annually, has to create customers in the same numbers. To push a particular automobile—which sometimes appears to differ little from a competitor's model—a manufacturer has to use Appeals to human desires, appeals that admittedly have little or nothing to do with the product itself. Sex and status are strong appeals. They are what the public wants—what we all want. As long as people will believe that sex appeal and status can come with a car, manufacturers will use these appeals to stay in competition and sell their product.

Keeping up with the modern scene, some automobile advertisers have added a "we care" touch and, particularly, use of Humor Appeals. We might like to think that this humor advertising shows we are getting more sophisticated. But humor is an old human appeal with three advertising advantages: (1) humor attracts a customer's attention, (2) humor is often repeated to friends and (3) the Humor Appeal flatters us because most of us want to believe we are too intelligent to be influenced by straight advertising appeals—despite statistics that say we are influenced.

An automobile advertiser like Volkswagen—whose product would not continue to sell if customers were not satisfied—not only uses very funny humor about the "Bug," but also implies that its customers are too bright to believe ordinary advertising and Volkswagen knows it. (And just happens to have a few million dollars to spend to amuse such intelligent people.)

Cosmetic advertising uses the same old Appeals, too. In the 1920's, Woodbury's Facial Soap showed a woman whose hand was being held by a lover, with the caption, "How long can a woman keep the charm of 'A skin you love to touch'?" Today Jergens Lotion advertises, "Would he hold hands with a cactus?"

In the 1920's, cigarette advertisers sought to double their customers by attracting women. They came up with such advertisements as a picture of a woman saying to an attractive man smoking a cigarette, "Blow a little my way," and with an admonition to a pretty, plump woman, "Reach for a Lucky instead of a Sweet." Candy manufacturers protested but had to increase their advertising appeals to stay in competition. Today, some cigarette advertisers try appeals to men and masculine pride by showing a rugged outdoors westerner and using the slogan, "Come to Marlboro Country."

Few, if any, ads today do not include propaganda devices. What Appeal, for example, lies in the following effective advertisement: "How did thirty-eight-year-old Ann Craig pass as a teen-ager? Creamy, mild Ivory Liquid gave her a hand." What was the pleasant, humorous Misleading Association that made both Campbell Soup and Alka Seltzer advertise by naming their product and then adding "on the rocks?" What Logical Fallacy—100 percent form—can be found in the popular newspaper advertisement: "Last Wednesday 25 jobs for maintenance men were advertised in the Gazette. How many can you find today?" Why does American Telephone and Telegraph Company not only try to explain why you may have been having difficulty with local phone calls lately but also put in big letters the Distraction advertisement, "We built Telstar but cut off your call to the hairdresser."

The United States citizen is exposed to an average of 2,000 advertisements daily, carried on match folders, cereal boxes, toothpaste tubes, store windows, bus signs, billboards, newspapers, magazines, circulars, radio, television—the list is almost endless. In 1968, according to the American Advertising Federation, about seventeen billion dollars, or about 2½ percent of the gross national product of the United States, were invested in advertising. Of the one hundred leading advertisers, more than ninety consistently spend ten million dollars or more each year. Such big advertisers as General Motors, Ford, Proctor and Gamble, American Home Products, to name only a few, have built into their advertising campaigns not only most of the common propaganda devices but also the most effective of the propaganda strategies: Repetition.

Of propaganda's common devices and stratagems, only the Name-calling Device and the Confusion Stratage. are seldom used in advertising. Modern advertisers generally avoid accusing their competitors of anything, and an advertiser normally does not want to confuse his customers about his product. Every other propaganda device is in use in advertising. Is the American public then being overwhelmed by economic propaganda? In a sense, yes. At least the public cannot prevent being exposed to it.

And, despite the Federal Trade Commission, the agency that "polices" illegal advertising, critics do occasionally accuse advertisers of deceiving the public. However, the advertising industry can easily prove the value of advertising. For example, toothpaste manufacturers do increase their sales by snappy Selective Slogans, Sex Appeals and Glittering Words about secret ingredients, even though most dentists maintain there is little real difference between the various toothpastes. Yet tooth care does have health importance. How many people would be using toothpaste regularly or insisting that their children brush their teeth, if it were not for the continual toothpaste advertising?

The advertising industry has an even more telling reply to critics. Strict control of advertising—and therefore control of the propaganda devices used—would inevitably result in control of free competition and would undercut our

American economy as we know it. In short, advertising that uses propaganda devices is here to stay. Much of the movement and competition of the American economy depends on it. In part, our country was built on such advertising. But where does all this leave us "unprotected" consumers? Well, we still have freedom of choice. We can be educated to detect propaganda appeals to our emotions rather than our reason. And we can, above all, decide for ourselves whether or not any given product is something we actually want and need.

However, economic propaganda only involves selling "things," and most economic propaganda campaigns are conducted by large groups of specially trained men and women. In the next chapter, we will see how one woman, untrained in propaganda techniques and working alone, managed to sell not a "thing" but a "belief." And by doing so, influenced the lives of thousands of her fellow Americans and helped change the course of history.

Social Propaganda: From Abolition to Prohibition

IN FEBRUARY of 1851, a thirty-nine-year-old housewife in Brunswick, Maine, sat down and began to write a story. This serialized story, later made into a book, was to do more to influence the minds and inflame the emotions of her countrymen than any piece of American writing since Thomas Paine's *Common Sense*. The woman was Harriet Beecher Stowe, and the book was *Uncle Tom's Cabin*.

Thomas Paine wrote his pamphlets deliberately to arouse the American colonists to the cause of freedom. Harriet Beecher Stowe wrote her book just as deliberately to win the American people to the abolitionist cause, "to make this whole nation feel what an accursed thing slavery is." It is doubtful if even Mrs. Stowe dreamed how successful she

147

would be. In its first year, *Uncle Tom's Cabin* sold more than 300,000 copies; and in the following years, the book was translated into nearly every European language. Millions of copies were sold in America and abroad.

Northern millhands and eastern city dwellers, the small town shopkeeper and the midwest farmer—many of whom had never met a black person in their lives and were only vaguely interested in or even indifferent to the plight of the Negro slave in America—read of the martyrdom and death of Uncle Tom and were moved to tears and righteous wrath against slavery and the Southern slaveholders. The popular stage play subsequently made from the book brought even more converts to the abolitionist cause.

Despite the worthiness of its cause, the book itself with its over-sentimentalized plot and stereotyped characters had little literary merit. It was, however, excellent propaganda. Like all good propaganda, it used strong Appeals to the Emotions of the reader, and employed other common devices such as Selected Truths parading as whole truths, Over-simplification, and Card Stacking. Uncle Thomas was presented as the most noble of men, and the plantation overseer Simon Legree as the most wicked.

Successful as *Uncle Tom's Cabin* was as propaganda—and there are historians who claim the book did more than anything else to unify public opinion in the north against slavery—the book was only one of many anti-slavery propaganda tracts, just as Harriet Beecher Stowe was only one of many abolitionists.

Between the years of 1830 and 1860, some 2,000 abolitionist societies were formed in the United States. Their sole purpose was to fan the smoldering issue of slavery to a white-hot blaze, to convince the North and South that slavery was a festering evil that must be abolished from the country.

The cause of the abolitionists, as many another cause

given force by propaganda, was, of course, good. Propaganda had to be used because balanced logic would not bring about the desired action. To read a quietly logical speech or article against slavery would not excite the emotions of workingmen, whose conditions often were not much better than those of the slaves.

The institution of slavery was evil. But people do not arouse easily against an established institution. Sympathetic emotional shock was needed, and so many an anti-slavery fighter used the Atrocity story.

As early as 1839, Theodore Weld, an early abolitionist, compiled and published a collection of stories about the brutality of slave life, called *American slavery as it is: testimony of a thousand witnesses.* The book sold a hundred thousand copies in its first year. Escaped slaves, like Frederick Douglass, William Wells Brown, Josiah Henson and Solomon Northrup wrote and had published, often with the assistance of abolitionist societies, their own accounts of the horrors of life for a slave in the deep South.

Anti-slavery periodicals, like the *Anti-Slavery Almanac,* were filled with tales of the bestiality of the Southern slaveholder toward his slaves. Pictures showed in gory detail the flogging and torture of men, women and children. Some of the early slave narratives were later revealed to be hoaxes, and undoubtedly there was some exaggeration of cruelty in others, but unfortunately there were more than enough true stories to compensate for the exaggeration.

In their publications, the abolitionists recognized the value of Card Stacking, of telling only one side of the story. *All* slaveholders were invariably cruel and brutal. Little, if any, mention was made of slaveholders who treated their slaves humanely, or of the fact that many of the slaves who did escape North often found as much discrimination there as in the South.

The anti-slavery fighters, however, did not rely on written

propaganda alone. Hundreds of fugitive slaves, supported by abolitionists (including funds from free black people), traveled through the free states, lecturing on the evils of slavery, often showing the scars of whippings on their own bodies. Some of these ex-slaves were such accomplished agitators that when they finished speaking, there wasn't a dry eye in the audience. People who had come out of curiosity to hear a black man or woman speak, left the hall convinced that slavery must be abolished.

White abolitionists like William Lloyd Garrison also took to the lecture circuit, speaking at churches, town meetings, wherever they could gain an audience. One particularly effective gesture Garrison used, which always brought a good deal of publicity and therefore propaganda for the cause (much as draft-card burning does today), was his public burning of a copy of the Constitution to show his contempt for a law that permitted slavery among free men.

Garrison was also the editor of the newspaper, the *Liberator,* probably the best known propaganda voice of the abolitionist cause. On the front page of the first issue of this paper, Garrison stated boldly: "On the subject [of slavery] I do not want to think or speak or write with moderation . . . I am in earnest . . . I will not equivocate, I will not excuse, I will not retreat a single inch . . . and *I will be heard!*"

Was all this anti-slavery propaganda effective? Apparently the South thought so. Southern governments leveled severe penalties on any person caught circulating or reading abolitionist literature. Men even suspected of handling such material were flogged and hanged. A South Carolina post office was invaded and bags of mail containing abolitionist propaganda were dragged out into the street and burned. An attempt was even made by Southerners to have a federal law passed that would force postmasters to censor and destroy any abolitionist literature.

In the North, pro-slavery men whose business interests depended on the friendship of the South, attacked abolitionists, jailing them. The editor of one abolitionist newspaper, Elijah Lovejoy, was shot and killed by an angry mob. Garrison, himself, was once almost lynched, and his newspaper had to go underground for a time.

The outpouring of abolitionist propaganda made people in the South feel the need for influencing public opinion in support of its "peculiar institution," as slavery was euphemistically called by the Southern slaveholders. The propaganda image of the slave they projected, and the attitude they wanted the North to accept, was one of a black man incapable of maintaining himself if freed; Southern propaganda purported that black people were irresponsible and shiftless and helpless without a master, that it was God's will that the black man be a slave.

To impress this image upon Northern minds, Southerners used the Testimonial Appeal, quoting from the Bible and drawing attention to the curse God placed upon the son of Ham: "Cursed be Canaan; a servant of servants shall he be unto his brethren." Since Bible readers of the nineteenth century believed that the black race descended from the sons of Ham, such propaganda seemed to prove that God himself had decreed that black people should be slaves.

Southerners used other Testimonial Appeals, also, not quite as exalted as the Bible. The pseudo-scientist, Dr. S. A. Cartwright, proved "scientifically" that "The Negro brain froze in a cold climate, inducing insanity, and therefore out of kindness to the Negro, he should be kept South."

Other well-known propagandists for slavery were Robert Barnwell Rhett, who published a pro-slavery newspaper, and George Fitzhugh, who wrote articles advocating slavery. These articles used words that have a familiar ring today. In his Fear Appeal, he claimed that if the abolitionists succeeded in freeing the slaves, it would be a "surrender to Socialism and to Communism . . . to no private property, no church, no law, to free love, free lands, free women and free children."

Perhaps the most effective piece of propaganda used by the South was the Misleading Association device. Through pictures and pamphlets sent throughout the free states, they compared the lot of the happy, contented slave, singing at his tasks under a kindly God-fearing master, to the lot of the wretched millworkers in New England who drudged long hours at little pay for indifferent, cruel employers.

Although it is doubtful that Southern propaganda had much effect in influencing public opinion for slavery in the free states, it did help to unify public opinion and arouse feelings of distrust and hatred in the South against the North— just as the abolitionist propaganda unified opinion and aroused emotions in the North against the South. Finally there was little common meeting ground between the two polarized opinions, for and against slavery, and the way was opened to Civil War.

Another social movement in the United States history that used propaganda devices extensively, was the temperance movement against alcohol. Abolitionists, like Henry Ward Beecher, considered the traffic in alcohol just as sinful and dishonorable as slavery, and often handed out propaganda tracts against demon rum at the same meetings that they spoke out against slavery.

Driving out liquor was not an easy task. The consumption of liquor, from homemade ciders and beer to imported rum and wines, had always been considered an inalienable right; it was an essential part of the social as well as economic life of early America. In the early days of the nation,

One of the most famous scenes from the stage play, *Uncle Tom's Cabin*, showing the slave, Eliza, and her child escaping across the frozen Ohio River with Simon Legree and a pack of bloodhounds in close pursuit. To the thousands of northerners who saw the play and read the book, the vicious Simon Legree became a symbol of the hated southern slave owner, and helped arouse bitter feelings against the Fugitive Slave Law passed in 1850. *The New York Historical Society, New York City*

EMANCIPATOR—*EXTRA.*

NEW-YORK, SEPTEMBER 2, 1839.

American Anti-Slavery Almanac for 1840.

The seven cuts following, are selected from thirteen, which may be found in the Anti-Slavery Almanac for 1840. They represent well-authenticated facts, and illustrate in various ways, the cruelties daily inflicted upon three millions of native born Americans, by their fellow-countrymen! A brief explanation follows each cut.

The peculiar "Domestic Institutions of our Southern brethren."

Selling a Mother from her Child.

Mothers with young Children at work in the field.

A Woman chained to a Girl, and a Man in irons at work in the field.

"They can't take care of themselves"; explained in an interesting article.

Slaves with dogs and guns. A Slave drowned

Servility of the Northern States in arresting and returning fugitive Slaves.

Anti-slavery Almanacs were published and circulated by the Abolitionists. The Almanacs described and pictured in lurid detail the sufferings of the slaves. *The Bettmann Archive, Inc.*

154

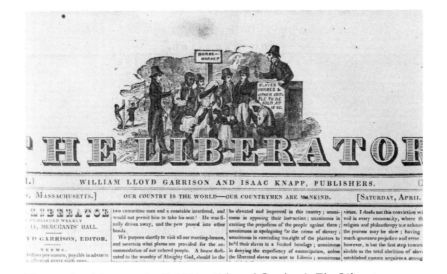

The masthead from an April, 1831, edition of Garrison's *The Liberator,*
showing an auction with "slaves, horses, and other cattle to be sold." This
weekly newspaper was a main propaganda weapon in the arsenal of the
Abolitionists. Many southerners felt that the slave uprising led by Nat Turner
in 1831 was caused, in part, by Garrison, and *The Liberator* was banned and
burned in the streets of the South. *The Liberator, April 23, 1831*

Frontispiece of one of the many
anti-slavery biographies written
by ex-slaves and published by
Abolitionists, using the Atrocity
Appeal to arouse the North
against the horrors of slavery.
*St. Louis Junior College District
Libraries*

NARRATIVES

OF THE SUFFERINGS OF

LEWIS AND MILTON CLARKE,

SONS OF A SOLDIER OF THE REVOLUTION,

DURING A

CAPTIVITY OF MORE THAN TWENTY YEARS

AMONG THE

SLAVEHOLDERS OF KENTUCKY,

ONE OF THE

SO CALLED CHRISTIAN STATES OF NORTH AMERICA.

DICTATED BY THEMSELVES.

BOSTON
PUBLISHED BY BELA MARSH,
NO 25 CORNHILL.
1846

All Orders to be sent to the Publisher.
PRICE, 25 CENTS.

To combat the anti-slavery fervor of Abolitionists in England as well as New England, the Misleading Association device was widely used by the pro-slavery forces, contrasting carefree, happy slaves in the south with miserable factory workers in England and the North. *Library of Congress*

This Currier and Ives lithograph, and other pictures of its type, helped support the pro-slavery propaganda that the southern slaves were not cruelly oppressed but instead were happy, childlike creatures passing their time singing and dancing, living in small, comfortable cabins near the plantation house. *Harry T. Peters Collection, Museum of the City of New York*

Even after the Civil War, the myth of the happy, carefree lives of the black people in the South persisted, as in this lithograph which appeared in *Harpers Weekly* in 1867, showing black fieldhands on Saturday night dancing before the big house for the plantation owner and his guests. *Harpers Weekly, February 2, 1867*

SATURDAY EVENINGS DANCE.

This poster, published in 1907 by the Anti-saloon League, uses the Testimonial Appeal of allegedly scientific statistics to advance the cause of prohibition. *Andrew Sinclair,* Prohibition (*Atlantic-Little, Brown*)

The Temperance leaders used exaggerated Appeals to Fear to persuade Americans to give up the bottle. They portrayed the descending "steps" of drinking: taking one glass, becoming a drunkard, falling into desperation and crime, and finally dying by suicide. *Library of Congress*

Defective Children
Increased With
ALCOHOLIZATION
of FATHERS

Among the Defects were Epilepsy, Feeble-mindedness and St. Vitus Dance

219 Children of Occasional Drinkers
2.3% DEFECTIVE

130 Children of Regular Moderate Drinkers
4.6% DEFECTIVE

67 Children of Regular Heavy Drinkers
9% DEFECTIVE

53 Children of Drunkards
19% DEFECTIVE

Alcoholism and Defects of Brain and Nerves Go Hand in Hand

Regular "Moderate" Drinkers Drank daily less than the equivalent of 2 qts. of Beer;Heavy Drinkers more than this amount.

THE DRUNKARD'S PROGRESS.

THE RAILROAD THAT LEADS FROM EARTH TO HELL.

The "A" to "Z" Railroad that led
from earth to hell was a favorite
device of the Temperance
groups to shown how a man
went from one bottle of ale (A)
to the crossroads of destruction
(X) until he became yoked (Y)
to the zero of hell (Z). *Library
of Congress*

The Women's Christian Temperance Union of 1874 staged
"Kneel-in's" in front of saloons
to protest use of liquor and
arouse public sentiment against
the evil of alcohol. *Brown
Brothers*

This Currier and Ives Print, 1869, uses some of the common points of ridicule against the women who sought votes and civil rights under the law. The women's rightists were depicted as ugly or frivolous, smoking cigars at the ballot box and making men carry the babies. Name-calling techniques, such as "Miss Hang Man for Sheriff," and "Vote for Susan Sharp Tongue," were typical propaganda to indicate that the idea of women's rights could not be taken seriously. *Library of Congress*

The *Life* magazine cover of 1910 continues the campaign of ridicule against women seeking civil rights. The two women in police uniforms are the usual propaganda Stereotypes of women's rightists. The caption under the picture reads, "Held by the Enemy." *Life magazine, September 15, 1910*

Frontispiece of a book published in 1900 using the Testimonial Appeal of the Bible and Name Calling to supposedly prove the supremacy of the white man and the inferiority of the black man. *St. Louis Junior College District libraries*

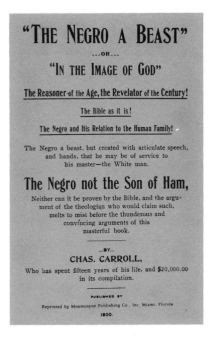

"THE NEGRO A BEAST"

...OR...

"IN THE IMAGE OF GOD"

The Reasoner of the Age, the Revelator of the Century!

The Bible as it is!

The Negro and His Relation to the Human Family!

The Negro a beast, but created with articulate speech, and hands, that he may be of service to his master—the White man.

The Negro not the Son of Ham,

Neither can it be proven by the Bible, and the argument of the theologian who would claim such, melts to mist before the thunderous and convincing arguments of this masterful book.

...BY...

CHAS. CARROLL,

Who has spent fifteen years of his life, and $20,000.00 in its compilation.

PUBLISHED BY

Reprinted by Mnemosyne Publishing Co., Inc. Miami, Florida

1900.

"Humorous" prints and pictures, such as this Currier and Ives lithograph of 1886, depicted the derogatory Stereotype of the black man. This print is from a series called "Darktown" that sold well. The Stereotype was a potent propaganda force against Afro-Americans achieving full civil rights and equality. *Harry T. Peters Collection, Museum of the City of New York*

GREAT OYSTER EATING MATCH BETWEEN THE DARK TOWN CORMORANT AND THE BLACKVILLE BUSTER.
The Finish —"Yous is a tie - De one dat gags fust. am a gone Coon."

Communist revolutionaries, using the militant Black masses, are at
this moment preparing for a terror-campaign in the city of St. Louis.
The racial attacks on our White people will be centered in St. Louis
starting early next year!

The honest White workers will suffer the arrogance of Black rabble-
rousers who demand high positions on the job line without earning
those positions. This criminal intrusion by a stupid, savage minority will slow construction in St. Louis and result in the loss of
employment for thousands of White working men.

The White youth will bare the brunt of Negro savagery in the high
schools, where the battle for our survival as a race is being determined.

WHITE PEOPLE! DO NOT allow yourselves to be terrorized! Stand now
against the storm of race-war and communist anarchy soon to come!
Only in a mighty unification of our disunited White people can we
hope to survive the terror and chaos soon to confront us.

****

AGAINST: Communism   FOR: U.S. Constitution

AGAINST: Black Revolution   FOR: White Power

AGAINST: Peace-Creep Treason   FOR: The Ressurrection of
                                        American Patriotism

****

NATIONAL SOCIALIST WHITE PEOPLE'S PARTY
P.O. Box 6168•Chicago, Illinois 60680

An example of the National Socialist White People's Party (Nazi) propaganda in the United States in the present day. Most prominent device is the
Fear Appeal (racial attacks, loss of jobs, danger to youth). But Name
Calling, Loaded Words, Glittering Generalities, and Misleading Association
devices are also present. *Authors' Collection*

(RIGHT) Today's followers of Hitler's creed of Aryan supremacy use the
same propaganda devices as the Nazi party did in Germany . . . picking a
scapegoat (the Communists and the black race) and appealing to fear and
"patriotism" to win converts. What is really being sold is disunity and racism.
Michael Choukas, Propaganda Comes of Age (*Public Affairs Press*)

HERE'S THE DOUBLE-TALK YOU GET FROM THE GOP

In the North, the GOP "Talks Tough" on Civil Rights:

"President Eisenhower's Republican Administration has registered the greatest advance for the rights of racial minorities since the Emancipation Proclamation . . . . Speaking for a unanimous Supreme Court, a great Republican Chief Justice, Earl Warren, has ordered an end to racial segregation in the nation's schools."
—*Vice President Nixon, New York, Feb. 13, 1956.*

. . . But In the South, the GOP Is "Moderate" on Civil Rights:

Charles K. McWhorter of New York, Young Republican National Chairman, speaking in Jackson, Miss., cited the Republican record as that of "a conservative party, moderate on 'civil rights' " . . . and went on to say that this "best suits the interest of Mississippians."—*Jackson (Miss.) States-Times, May 25, 1956.*

COMPARE THE RECORDS — AND MAKE YOUR CHOICE

What President Truman Did

Developed a comprehensive 10-point civil-rights program in 1948, and pressed for Congressional action on it EVERY YEAR until he left office.

What President Eisenhower Failed To Do

Presented no civil-rights program to Congress during his first 3½ years in office; failed to support Democratic civil-rights bill in 1955; waited until election year to present program—a watered-down version of Democratic proposals.

What The GOP Promised

The 1952 GOP Platform promised—

• Federal anti-lynch legislation.

• Federal anti-poll-tax legislation.

• Fair employment practices (FEPC) law.

What The GOP Did

President Eisenhower—

• Failed to support Democratic anti-lynch legislation in 1955; failed to mention anti-lynch legislation in 1956 GOP program.

• Failed to support Democratic anti-poll-tax bill in 1955; failed to mention anti-poll-tax legislation in 1956 GOP program.

• Personally opposed FEPC legislation and failed to mention FEPC in 1956 program.

The 1956 REPUBLICAN Platform

The 1956 Platform represents a major retreat from the GOP's 1952 pledges. It mainly lists GOP civil-rights "achievements," but it contains—
No pledge on the right to vote.
No pledge on non-discrimination in employment.
No pledge on security of the person.

The 1956 DEMOCRATIC Platform

"The Democratic Party pledges itself to continue its efforts to eliminate illegal discriminations of all kinds, in relation to
"(1) full rights to vote,
"(2) full rights to engage in gainful occupations,
"(3) full rights to enjoy security of the person..."

Both party Platforms recognize the Supreme Court decision on school desegregation as the law of the land, and the Democratic Platform specifically pledges continuing efforts to eliminate all discrimination as to "full rights to education in all· publicly supported institutions."

From a 1956 leaflet of the National Democratic Committee.

**This is the Symbol of
MY FAITH**

The CROSS is the symbol of Western, Christian civilization.

I believe America was founded as a CHRISTIAN Nation, and nobody has a right to destroy that tradition of the majority.

**This is the Symbol of
MY COUNTRY**

My ancestors fought and died to establish our blessed American Constitutional REPUBLIC.

I believe we have the right to KEEP it a REPUBLIC, not a race—mixing Democracy as the Reds preach.

**This is the Symbol of
MY RACE**

....My WHITE Race. The swastika was first used by the White Conquerors who brought civilization to India, the Aryans. Because I love my WHITE RACE, it does not mean I hate other races. But I DO hate what some "minority" groups are DOING to my White Christian America. Forced and hypocritical race-mixing helps NOBODY but the Communists, who want chaos and upheaval

FOR INFORMATION WRITE:

AMERICAN NAZI PARTY
POST OFFICE BOX 1381 • ARLINGTON, VA.

Bumper stickers are a favorite American way of proclaiming beliefs. Almost invariably they appear in the form of the Over-simplification device (slogans) and Appeal to Emotion, not logic. The "America—Love It or Leave It" sloganeers imply those who oppose government policies (such as the Vietnam War) are treasonous. "Americans for Peace" sloganeers imply that those who do not favor immediate withdrawal from Vietnam are war-lovers. *Authors' Collection*

This pamphlet cover uses the Logical Fallacy—Hot-Potato approach. (The question cannot be answered without accepting the assumption that there is communism in the National Council of Churches.) The National Council of Churches is an organization representing most of the Protestant churches in the United States. The pamphlet attempts to show that many clergymen members have aided Communist causes. *Courtesy of Laymen's Commission of The American Council of Christian Churches, P.O. Box 8775, Pittsburgh, Pa.*

HOW RED IS THE NATIONAL COUNCIL OF CHURCHES?

READ THE **FACTS** INSIDE AND DRAW YOUR OWN CONCLUSIONS

Americans felt so strongly about their right to liquor that one of the first examples of civil disobedience in the United States was the Whisky Rebellion; a group of Pennsylvanians rebelled against a federal excise tax on liquor.

Nevertheless, as early as 1826, the American Society for the Promotion of Temperance was formed; and in 1833, the United States Temperance Union was organized. Soon hundreds of similar groups sprang up around the country, all with one aim in mind: to persuade the American people that drinking alcohol was morally wrong and should be legally abolished from the country.

The basic propaganda device used by the temperance movement was an Appeal to Fear: one sip of liquor would turn a person into a confirmed drunkard; one casual drink meant dishonor and ruin for family and friends, disease and a horrible death for the drinker. Not only would the drinker destroy himself and his family, but his children would be born idiots.

The Bandwagon Appeal was also used effectively. Nondrinkers, as well as drinkers, were urged to sign the Pledge, promising never to touch a drop of liquor. Everyone else in town was signing the Pledge. Why not you? Signing the Temperance Pledge became a mark of prestige, of status in a community. Politicians signed the Pledge to get votes; young men signed the Pledge to get their young ladies to agree to marry them. Some Pledge signers were undoubtedly won over by this temperance propaganda. However, many publicly signed the Pledge and privately continued drinking.

Then, in 1854, Timothy Arthur, one of the foremost propagandists for the temperance cause, wrote his book, *Ten Nights in a Bar Room,* which became almost as famous as *Uncle Tom's Cabin.* The play made from the book, entitled *The Drunkard,* with its melodramatic emotional appeal on the evils of drink, ranked second only to *Uncle Tom's Cabin* in popularity.

After the Civil War, a new interest in and respect for science arose in the United States. Science and scientists were admired, and temperance workers grasped upon another propaganda device—the Testimonial Appeal. The results of medical research (using what was said to be scientific data) were widely published by temperance societies, displaying in full color and vivid detail the corrosive effects of alcohol upon the human body. "Foremost scientists" and "the greatest living authority" were quoted freely, even if the scientists were obscure and unknown. Statistics, supposedly based upon scientific fact, were published to prove the disastrous effects of alcohol—probably the first appearance in American propaganda history of statistics being used in this fashion.

All such medical research and statistics were, of course, carefully screened. Only the research and statistics that showed the terrible effect of taking even one drink were "selected" for propaganda use. Any research that found no fault in moderate drinking was eliminated.

This careful selection process was so effective that there were thousands upon thousands of Americans in the nineteenth century, who, because of such temperance propaganda, sincerely believed that science had proven that a drunkard could catch fire from his own breath and be burned alive; that all children of anyone who took even one drink would be born defective; and that the stomach of anyone who drank turned black.

American women, who had always been in the forefront of the temperance movement, formed the Women's Christian Temperance Union. Although unable to vote themselves, W.C.T.U. members were able to place such pressure on state legislators that anti-alcohol propaganda entered the schoolroom. In many states, laws were passed requiring textbooks to carry lurid pictures of black stomachs and pickled brains—the inevitable results of drinking—and frightening tales of children with weak minds born of a parent who drank.

Outside of the schoolroom, children were organized into Cold Water Armies, which marched in pre-election parades waving flags and placards that read: "When we can vote, the saloon will go." "Tremble, King Alcohol, we shall grow up!"

This "struggle for the children's minds," as the W.C.T.U. described it, was important because it was this captive audience who, when they were grown, became some of the strongest supporters for prohibition.

The more aggressive of the W.C.T.U. members broke into saloons and smashed furniture and bars. More conservative women temperance workers aroused public opinion against saloons by conducting the first "kneel-ins." The women would kneel and pray before a saloon for days on end, discouraging customers until the saloon owner was forced to close his business.

Of all the temperance organizations, the Anti-Saloon League formed in 1893 was the most successful. It established a chain of command leading from its headquarters (and a strong lobby) in Washington, D.C., down to 50,000 field workers at state level. Within fourteen years, the league had printed and distributed so many pamphlets, books, posters and free clipsheets to newspapers, in addition to temperance journals and magazines, that someone said, "prohibition propaganda fell thicker than hailstones on the heads of the people." By the early 1900's, it was almost impossible to pick up a newspaper or magazine without reading an article or editorial that made alcohol the chief scapegoat for everything that was wrong with the country, from poverty and crime, to disease and socialism. Prohibition was presented, of course, as the cure-all for every social ill.

Finally, with the coming of World War I, and the resulting hatred of all things German, the prohibitionists were able to seize upon an almost infallible Appeals Propaganda Device: the Appeal to Patriotism. Most of the brewing companies in the country were owned by people of German extraction. Therefore, any supporters of the wets and drinking were automatically unpatriotic, traitors and partisans of the Kaiser and the Huns.

As one league pamphlet pointed out: "The time has come for a division between those who are for German beer drinkers and those who are for the loyal drys . . . for the unquestioned and undiluted American patriots, or slackers and enemy sympathizers." And in a final burst of Name Calling, the time had come "to abolish the Un-American, pro-German, crime-producing, food-wasting, youth-corrupting, home-wrecking, treasonable liquor traffic."

On a wave of such patriotic propaganda, by 1917 the Eighteenth Amendment was well on its way to ratification. By 1920 prohibition of liquor was the law of the land. All over the country, prohibitionists rejoiced at the news. Temperance workers forecast a new era where no jails, asylums or poorhouses would be needed. "Hell," one triumphant prohibitionist declared, "would now be for rent!"

As it turned out, the celebrations were a little premature. However desirable and well intentioned, prohibition did not eliminate all social evils from the land. Although the drys had been highly effective with their propaganda, almost immediately after the passage of the Eighteenth Amendment, their propaganda began to backfire. As one historian explained, "Propaganda was the Frankenstein of the drys. At first, it was their power and glory; but at last, it murdered its maker."

168

The drys had made alcohol the scapegoat for all that was wrong with America. The wets now used this same device to destroy the drys. After World War I, and the passage of prohibition, the country went through an era of depression and economic disaster, and a rise in bootlegging, racketeering and crime in the streets. That these developments were not all the direct result of prohibition did not matter. The wets triumphantly made the drys the scapegoat for all the problems facing America, from unemployment to a rise in the crime rate and a lowering of moral standards.

The wets borrowed other propaganda devices from the drys. They subsidized and published their own scientific research studies and used them as Testimonial Appeals, proving that alcohol, when used in moderation, was not as deadly as the drys had claimed. When the American Medical Association in 1922 reversed its stand and declared that alcohol, after all, did have a therapeutic value, the wets pounced on this gleefully as further "scientific proof" that alcohol was not dangerous.

In addition, the wets appealed to the middle-class American's most vulnerable point—his pocketbook—pointing out the cost in tax dollars of trying to enforce prohibition, and the millions of dollars lost in federal revenue with the elimination of the liquor tax.

The wets even used Name Calling to their advantage. The Anti-Saloon League became "the mightiest engine of propaganda the world has ever beheld" and the claim was made that the drys were trying to run the "government by propaganda." Then, as today, the word "propaganda" had enough Scare Appeal to make many Americans begin to fear for loss of personal liberties.

But probably the main reason the dry propaganda began to fail after the passage of the Eighteenth Amendment was that the propaganda had far overreached itself. The drys had promised America a new utopia with prohibition, a promise they were, of course, not able to fulfill. As prohibition promises proved false; as the scientific claims of the drys proved inaccurate; the wets turned upon the drys the last blow—the propagandic device of ridicule. Prohibition became the butt of jokes in cartoons and in magazines, in newspapers and over the radio.

The final outcome was the repeal of the Eighteenth Amendment. But there were other side effects. Many people, weary and disillusioned by both the wet and dry propaganda, became cynical about all reform movements. And, perhaps most important, with all the controversy stirred up by the propaganda of the drys and wets, many necessary and vital reforms needed in America were delayed or pushed aside altogether.

There was, however, one outcome of both the abolitionist and prohibitionist movements that could not have been foreseen. The American woman, who was extremely active in both these movements, began using the propaganda devices she had learned to achieve her own goal: shaping public opinion to bring about votes for women.

The early suffragists used the same time-tested propaganda devices and materials they had employed against slavery and prohibition: Appeals to Emotion in pamphlets; propaganda tracts; pro-suffragist articles planted in newspapers; street parades; catchy Slogans; formation of an effective lobby in Washington, D.C., to pressure legislators; and organizations with branches all over the country to provide funds to distribute suffragist propaganda. Despite the tremendous obstacle of sexual prejudice, a more difficult obstacle even than racial prejudice, the suffragists finally triumphed in 1920 with the passage of the Nineteenth Amendment giving women the right to vote. But not without great cost—because of the propaganda devices used against them. The strongest device was the Appeal of Ridicule, the kind of humor that is used to cut an opponent "down to size" and make him—in this case, her—a figure of fun. The effectiveness of this propaganda can still be seen today. The women who fought for women's suffrage were some of the most respected and intelligent women of their day. So successful, however, was the propaganda of ridicule used against them, so widespread and merciless was it, that even to this day the picture of the "suffragette" and "feminist" is a caricature—an ugly, mannish figure, often in big bloomers and smoking a cigar—a figure of fun in the public mind.

Out of this ridicule and its grotesque stereotype came fear. Any woman, and any man, too, fears being a figure of fun. Partly because of this fear, the suffragist movement progressed very slowly even after the vote was won. Only today are women really beginning to achieve the removal of unequal laws and discriminatory social customs between sexes.

Other hangovers from propaganda of the past still shape attitudes in our present society. Some modern day attitudes toward black people in America can be traced back to both abolitionist and pro-slavery propaganda. Mrs. Stowe's character Uncle Tom has become a stereotype and a name today for a submissive, meek Negro. The Stereotype of the shiftless, lazy black man presented by pro-slavery propaganda is still accepted by many white people today.

Propaganda downgrading blacks unfortunately did not stop with the Civil War. After the war, although freed from slavery, the black man was usually left homeless, poor, unable to read or write and untrained for any except the lowest jobs. The racially prejudiced said this was his natural state. Supposedly scientific research was used as Testimonial Appeal to "prove" that the black man was inherently inferior. In textbooks, some of them still used today, the propaganda

171

device of Selection was used to ignore the harsh facts of slavery and the accomplishments of black people, leaving the impression that they had been of little importance in American history.

Newspapers and even some of the better magazines of the late 1800's—*Harper's, Atlantic Monthly, Century*—used jokes and cartoons in which Name-Calling words like "coon," "darky," "pickaninny" and "nigger" were commonplace. Novels of the day like *The Leopard's Spots* and the *Clansman* by Thomas Dixon presented the black man as little more than a vicious beast. Even the famous early movie, *The Birth of a Nation,* inflamed public opinion against the black man. Almost up to the present day, movies used black characters as servants of the Uncle Tom type or presented them as humorous creatures of low mental ability.

Today the Ku Klux Klan, the White Citizens Council and other far-right organizations still spread their propaganda of white supremacy, deliberately trying to influence the minds and emotions of white people against the black.

An anti-Negro leaflet recently distributed in St. Louis by the National Socialist White People's Party (formerly the American Nazi Party), for example, uses the most blatant propaganda devices. It calls black people "black rabble-rousers" and a "stupid, savage minority"; and in an Appeal to Fear much like the ones Adolf Hitler used, it says, "White people, do not allow yourself to be terrorized. Stand now against the storm of race war and communist anarchy soon to come."

To combat this type of propaganda, the National Association for the Advancement of Colored People, formed in 1909, began publishing its own materials and propaganda, not only in an attempt to change the opinions of white people toward black, but to arouse in the black man a pride in his own race. One of the founders of the NAACP, William

E. B. DuBois, lectured widely throughout the United States, trying to arouse the nation to the plight of black people. In addition, he encouraged research into history so that historic facts could be used to present a more favorable picture of the black man's history and abilities. DuBois was also instrumental in beginning the publication of *The Crisis,* a magazine that became the principal means of information and propaganda of the NAACP.

These early efforts by the NAACP were met most often with indifference or outright resistance, because information in itself does not arouse emotions and even forceful propaganda can seldom operate effectively when the climate of opinion is strongly against the ideas it is fostering. However, in the 1950's and 1960's, the Civil Rights movement gained strength with the great growth of mass communication and the economic advance of black people. The propaganda appeals used by black groups today, such as the Appeals to Fear of the black militants, with their slogan of Black Power, as well as the "Prestige" Appeals of the "Black is beautiful" campaign, are deliberately designed to unify the black people and overcome the effects of the "white superiority" propaganda in the minds of black people.

Racial problems, however, are only one of the social issues facing the United States today in which propaganda is playing its role. There is the split between the far left—the radical students, the ultra-liberals—and the far right—the Birchites, Wallace supporters and other ultra-conservative groups. Both sides use all the standard propaganda devices. The Appeal to Fear: from the ultra-right, "The Communists are trying to take over our country," and from the ultra-left, "The Fascists are trying to destroy our country." Both sides use Appeals to Patriotism and the symbol of the American flag in such slogans as the far right's "America, love it or leave it" (anyone critical of America is automatically unpatriotic), and the far left's "Americans for Peace" (only the far left wants peace, so the far right automatically wants war).

The far right's Scapegoat is Communism; the far left's is the "racist, imperialist, power structure." Name Calling on both sides is, of course, endless, and like the selected Scapegoats, serves only to arouse prejudice without presenting any proof or documentation.

Another commonly used propaganda approach used by both sides is the 100–percent Approach. Thus, if, say 2 percent of those participating in a student riot profess Communism, the rightist forces say "Communist rioting" (100 percent). Or if a single policeman hits a student then, "All policemen are brutal pigs" (100 percent).

In the middle of these two forces sits the great body of indifferent, uncertain, confused or neutral Americans. It is this middle ground that both extremes are trying to win with their propaganda. As long as neither side's propaganda is strong enough to take over this great middle majority—or as long as most Americans refuse to accept the propaganda Stereotypes with which extremists tag a racial, political or religious group—or as long as Americans can solve social problems through reasonable discussion and compromise rather than Appeals to Prejudice and Hate—then a balance will be kept.

However, if either the extreme left or extreme right should capture the emotions and opinions, or shape the attitudes of this middle section, then the path of United States history could be dramatically altered.

Propaganda on the International Scene: Cut-off at the Culture Gap

IN THE EARLY stages of the war in Vietnam, the North Vietnamese Communist radio often beamed messages in English to the American troops: "Greetings, poor soldier lackeys of imperialists of America. Ten of your comrades were killed today near Bien Hoa, only a few miles from Saigon. . . . Give up this war for the racist Johnson. Go home to your loved ones and your fields."

These early propaganda efforts of Radio Hanoi had little influence because words like *lackeys* were foreign, and going home to "your fields" sounded funny to most American ears. An international propagandist cannot afford to have such culture gaps in his messages.

Of all types of propaganda, international propaganda—

propaganda that tries to influence the beliefs and actions of people of another country—is the most difficult. The international propagandist must know propaganda techniques and communication media—*and* he must also know his foreign audience. He must be aware of their attitudes toward their own government as well as his government, and know how they feel about neighboring lands. Most important, the propagandist must be aware of the culture gap between nations—he must realize that customs, morals, words, even colors, have different meanings in different countries.

A difference in standard of living can create a culture gap. When the Voice of America beamed broadcasts to Russia about commonplace labor-saving devices found in many American homes—telephones, clothes dryers and dishwashers—the Russian audiences laughed. The Russians simply did not believe the truth, because the truth could not, to them, be "true." The Russian woman could not imagine that such luxuries were available to an average American housewife, and therefore dismissed the whole broadcast as a lie. On the other hand, many Americans refused to believe, despite scientific proof, that Russian scientists had put men into space ahead of us. It had to be Russian "propaganda."

Thus, international propaganda must be less concerned with truth than with selecting facts or information that a foreign audience will believe out of its own experience. In Southeast Asia, Chinese herbs and acupuncture are more widely accepted as cures for illness than Western medicine. Why? Because Southeast Asians know that the Chinese people are more numerous than any other people in the world, and they also know that the Chinese nation has lasted longer than any other nation—so naturally its medicine must be better! On the other hand, most Americans believe their nation has the best medical care in the world. Yet, United Nations statistics show that infant mortality is greater in the

United States and life-span and availability of medical care lower than in many nations of Europe. We are all influenced by our cultures—and the international propagandist must move carefully across the gaps.

Foreign propaganda, particularly in war, is not new, of course. We can recall Benjamin Franklin in France writing pamphlets, letters and newspaper articles to convince the people of Europe that the American Revolution was just and necessary. The great French general Napoleon used foreign propaganda. He even bought a British newspaper and used it to influence the British people in his favor. Adolf Hitler, so successful with propaganda in his own country, tried in the 1930's and 1940's to spread his propaganda in the United States through radio broadcasts and Nazi front organizations. Examples of foreign propaganda are plentiful in history.

But for most Americans today, the words "foreign propaganda" suggests Communist propaganda, usually that of the Soviet Union or China. In fact, the first truly international propaganda did come from the Soviet Union. As early as 1902, the Russian Communist leader Lenin recognized the crucial influence of international propaganda. One of the first offices he created in his new organization was the Propaganda and Agitation Office. Its mission was not only to convert the people of Russia but to convert all of the peoples of the world to Communism. No matter how widespread the Communist propaganda became, however, the devices used remained the same. Here are a few examples out of multitudes:

Name Calling and Loaded Words: Americans in words and caricatures are invariably "racists," "imperialists" or "warmongers," guilty of "barbarous aggression."

Glittering Words: Communist front organizations are called such names as the World Peace Council and the Inter-

177

national Institute for Peace. The Stockholm Conference "peace" petition circulated to almost every nation of the world in the 1950's was Communist-inspired to discredit actions of the United States. A glittering image, the dove, an international symbol of peace, is displayed prominently in Communist paintings, parades and publicity materials.

The Hot-potato Logical Fallacy: Has a race riot occurred in Chicago? The National Guard is sent in to stop the violence. As an incident reported in world newspapers, this is bad publicity for the United States. But the Communist propagandist does not stop there. His approach is, "When are American militarists going to stop oppressing the black people?" This is the Hot-potato Approach, similar to the question, "When are you going to stop beating your wife?" No matter what answer is given, the effect is damaging.

The 100–percent Logical Fallacy: An American government official, speaking solely out of his own emotions and giving only his own opinion, says, "The United States should use the atom bomb on Hanoi." Few in the United States take him seriously, but Soviet propagandists quote him as "a representative of the American government" and therefore his words seem to represent the United States government's 100–percent attitude. Would a government representative dare to say this otherwise? In quite a few countries to which the Communist propaganda is beamed, the answer is no.

This 100–percent Logical Fallacy has certain other advantages for the Soviet propagandist. The Soviet government at once becomes the hero. For who else can stop the United States government from carrying out its bullying threat against Hanoi? (Of course, there is no possibility of the threat's being carried out, since the single official's statement does not represent the view of the American government as a whole.)

The Scapegoat: Have French grape growers had a bad

year? No matter what the reasons, blame the "ruthless American capitalists" with their American product Coca-Cola, which floods the European market and ruins wine merchants.

Are farmers in Latin America starving and having poor crops because of outmoded agricultural methods and unequal distribution of land? Blame the "Yankee imperialists" who are rich and have become so by exploiting Latin Americans and causing their problems.

Although the Soviet Communists were the first to use these common devices on an international scale, they are not unique in their use of them today. We Americans use the word "Communist" as a Name-calling Device; we choose the name "Peace Corps" for a volunteer international organization of our own; and whenever there is a riot against poverty or racism or inequities in the United States, what Scapegoat is most often blamed? Yes, the Communists.

The Soviet Communists remain unique in their use of one of the propaganda strategies, however. All propaganda uses Repetition Strategy, but only the Soviet Communists have used the Confusion Strategy in international propaganda. Soviet radio and news sources accuse the United States of vicious actions everywhere in the world. The accusations, loud and angry, last one day, one week, maybe one month. Then without warning the Soviet propaganda changes and becomes extremely friendly to the United States, with offers of cultural exchanges, compromises, cooperation. Just as suddenly come new demands, or perhaps sudden silence and inaction, or harsh dogmatic statements about the aims of the Soviet Union. These are followed by uncertain periods of apparent indifference, or neutrality, or suggested co-existence.

The Confusion Strategy makes it impossible to predict

179

at any one time what the official Soviet attitude will be and keeps other governments off balance in any attempts to deal with the Soviet Union. Such manipulation of information is, of course, only possible in a country like the Soviet Union, where all foreign—outgoing—information is controlled by the government. It would be impossible for the United States to use the Confusion Strategy.

When the Chinese Communists entered the international propaganda field, they copied many of the common devices used by the Russians. The United States became the Scapegoat in Asia. The former Chinese Vice-Premier Chen Yi used both Name Calling and the Scapegoat device when he made the following statements:

"The Imperialist United States is blocking friendlier relations between Japan and China."

"The Imperialist United States is using Asians as guinea pigs for testing of experimental weapons [in Vietnam]. The atomic bomb was used against Japan [Asians] but not against Germany [Europeans].

In 1956, Radio Peking began broadcasting its propaganda in Africa. The Name Calling and Scapegoat devices were still used; but, with an eye to the new audience, the propagandists pointed to the murders of Malcolm X and Martin Luther King and to other examples of racial unrest as typical of American government attitudes toward black peoples. The Communists in Vietnam Name-call Americans, "*white* murderers waging war on the weak *colored* people of Vietnam." [italics—author's]

Today, Communist China is second only to the Soviet Union in the number of propaganda broadcasts it makes weekly. (Egypt ranks third.) The United States' Voice of America ranks fourth. The Communist radio of Hanoi and Peking, as well as the radio broadcasts of the United States, reach regularly into remote villages in Vietnam, where only

"I am the State!"

"We are the State!"

A Russian view of capitalism and communism appearing in the official Russian humor magazine *Krokodil*. *Krokodil's* humor, though distributed in excerpts abroad, is basically aimed at the Russian people, upholding communism and downgrading capitalism. *William Nelson,* Out of the Crocodile's Mouth (*Public Affairs Press*)

This picture from *Krokodil* shows a fat little capitalist American (lower left) bragging about the food and luxuries in the United States to a tall, lean American working man who has a placard on his back reading "Five million Unemployed." *Krokodil,* the official Russian humor magazine, is circulated throughout Russia. *William Nelson,* Out of the Crocodile's Mouth (*Public Affairs Press*)

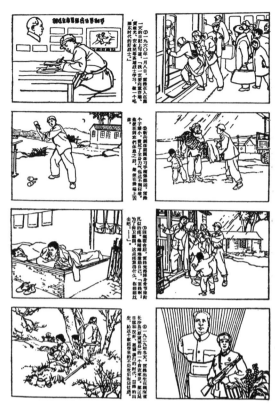

Chinese Communist comic strip used to influence Chinese and other Communist peoples. In the left strip, above, Lei Feng, Communist hero, is writing a "diary" in which he expresses his love of the new China under communism, with scenes of Chinese military preparedness. In the right strip, Lei Feng is shown coming to the assistance of various people and standing heroically in front of a statue of Mao Tsetung, leader and god-figure of the new China.
The U.S. Information Agency has also used comic or cartoon books on a worldwide basis, including biographies of famous Americans, to tell America's story abroad. *Michael Choukas,* Propaganda Comes of Age (*Public Affairs Press*)

Two typical front covers of the official Communist China magazine, *The Peking Review,* in 1968 and 1970. Published in Peking and heavily propagandistic, the magazine is distributed to English–speaking peoples. Although relations between the United States and Communist China may improve in the future, the national political approaches to influence other nations will not necessarily change. *The Peking Review*

United States Information Service Library, Katmandu, Nepal. These libraries, located in most of the countries of the world, have been visited by millions of foreign peoples. *United States Information Agency*

Russians at a newsstand in Moscow, buying copies of USIA's Russian-language magazine with title that means, in English, *America Illustrated. United States Information Agency*

Burmese looking at a window display in the U.S. Information Agency
Center in Rangoon, Burma. Window-displays in 176 U.S. Information
Centers abroad have proved an effective way of helping tell about life in the
United States—science, education, labor, agriculture—as well as help-
ing to explain United States foreign policies. *United States Information
Agency*

The Master Control of the Voice of America can tap 100 sources, send 26
radio programs to transmitters at once. Radio, far better than television or
print, can reach across national borders. *United States Information Agency*

This United States Information Agency poster-leaflet, in color, points out to the Thai people the difference between religion under communism and religion as a free people. *Library of Congress*

Distributed to the people of Thailand, this United States Information Agency poster-leaflet, in color, shows the difference between education as it exists under Chinese communism and education as it exists in a free democracy.
Library of Congress

Anti-American poster in Peking, China, in the late 1960's. This poster, a caricature of the then-U.S. President Johnson holding a bomb and being choked by many ropes, is one of many such posters attacking United States as "imperialist" and as only a "paper tiger" when faced by the Communist people's united effort. President Nixon's visit to Peking in 1972 was aimed partly at establishing better relations between the two countries. It is reported that during his visit the more virulent anti-American posters were removed or covered with thick red paint. *Marc Riboud Agence Magnum*

186

Wall posters in Shanghai, China. The Chinese people receive much of the latest political information—as well as propaganda—from such posters. Mao Tse-tung's picture (top left) is always prominently displayed. Intense propaganda campaigns can be carried on by the concentration and selection of information given to the Chinese people. *Hsinhua, New China News Agency, Peking*

The *Peking People's Daily,* leading newspaper of Communist China, in early March, 1972, put pictures of Chinese Chairman Mao and U.S. President Nixon on its front page—telling the Chinese people "officially" that they were to welcome President Nixon. Nixon and other American leaders, until a short time before, had been Name-called "warmongers" and "imperialists" by Chinese propagandists. Unlike newspapers in free countries, Communist newspapers always follow the official "line," allowing a concentration of propaganda without dissenting voices bringing up questions. *Peking People's Daily*

two Vietnamese in ten may read a newspaper but eight in ten will listen to or hear about radio broadcasts. In neighboring Cambodia, radio sets are usually found in village Buddhist wats (churches) and the messages, repeated by the bonzes (clergy) to the people, are therefore given high prestige. The information given on such radio broadcasts tends to over-simplify situations, to give easy answers. Thus, Americans—white, Western strangers—can be easily portrayed as "plotting war" against Asians, while the Chinese and North Vietnamese Communists are always "striving for peace."

Chinese and Soviet propagandists have not relied only on radio, of course. Both continually pour out a deluge of printed materials—books, pamphlets, tracts, posters. In one year, the Soviet Union published forty million copies of books in thirty-four languages for distribution throughout the world. This number does not include millions of books published within foreign countries by Communist-run presses. Meanwhile, China published more than ten million copies of books in sixteen free-world languages.

These are not dull political tracts. A young boy in Tibet learns to read by using the only textbook available to him—a Chinese published textbook, written to indoctrinate the student into Communist beliefs. A farmhand in Latin America learns to repair a tractor by using a Soviet repair manual. Children's comic books make up a big part of Communist printed propaganda and are gobbled up as eagerly by foreign children as comic books are by American children. In this printed material, any opponents of Communism are enemies of the "common people," and the Communists, of course, are always "friends of the common people."

Whether distributed by radio, printed material, trade fairs, movies, art exhibits, television or student exchanges, the international propaganda of Communist nations all carries the same intent: to influence world opinion in their favor. That also means making capitalism—and particularly the United States—a villain.

Until 1953, the United States did little to combat this distorted image. The information agency of the United States government had been operating as a stepchild of the State Department. But diplomats work with the high echelons of government; propaganda works among the people. Diplomacy and propaganda do not walk well hand in hand.

Then, in 1953, the United States Information Agency became an independent agency of the executive branch, responsible directly to the President. Its radio network retained the World War II name, "Voice of America." Today, although the Department of Defense and some semi-governmental agencies (such as Radio Free Europe) have radio broadcasting and visual facilities, the USIA remains the United States' most important international information agency.

Note that it is an "information" agency. President Kennedy in 1963 described one of the missions of the USIA as being to help "achieve United States foreign policy objectives by influencing public attitudes in other nations." The word "propaganda" is never used in referring to USIA work. Evidently "influencing public attitudes" has a more harmless sound to the American ear than "propaganda." Yet, propaganda has as its aim exactly that: influencing attitudes.

To accomplish its world-wide mission, the USIA uses a variety of media. USIA libraries in ninety-eight countries provide books and information about the United States and its people. These library information centers are so successful that when diplomatic relations falter, a USIA library often is attacked first by anti-American forces within the country. The attacks, although undoubtedly not appreciated by the librarians, are a kind of reverse tribute to the library's importance as a symbol of the United States.

The USIA also has printed and circulated abroad three million copies of trade and textbooks in English and in twenty foreign languages. Thirty-eight magazines are published in twenty-seven languages. The most important of these magazines is *America Illustrated* distributed in the Soviet Union. By a special reciprocal agreement with the Soviets, a counterpart magazine *Soviet Life* is distributed within the United States. Leaflets, pamphlets, printed exhibits and posters—even comic strips—are distributed in over one hundred countries. There is material suited to people in every walk of life.

The American exhibit at Expo '70 in Osaka, Japan, was created by USIA as were more than 150 other smaller traveling exhibits. One of the most successful, "Education-U.S.A.," which included samples of rocks brought from the moon, was visited by a million Soviet citizens.

The most effective medium of the USIA, however, is radio broadcasting. The Voice of America is the only way of reaching the people in some Communist-controlled nations. Many Soviet citizens first learned about the growing dissent among Soviet intellectuals and scientists by listening to the VOA. Although both the Soviet Union and Communist China continually attempt to jam VOA broadcasts, it is estimated that VOA broadcasting regularly reaches more than 50 million adults each week, and as many as 750 million when it reports on such outstanding events as the American Apollo 11 moon landing.

Television and film are, of course, the newest media used by USIA, which produces and acquires about 500 film and TV documentaries each year. These range from how-to-do-it educational films to films that show the evils of Communism as opposed to the virtues of capitalism and the American way of life. Films are especially useful in reaching remote areas where the literacy rate is low and other forms of communication are practically non-existent. Television is, of course, becoming increasingly important as a way of reaching into homes around the world. The USIA has already begun transmitting television programs by communications satellite and can be in immediate contact with an enormous foreign audience at almost the same moment an event—or U.S. policy decision—is being made.

Yet, in spite of all that the USIA has accomplished, there are several reasons why it has never been and probably never can be as effective as Communist propaganda agencies.

1. Lack of money. The budget of USIA is less than General Motors spends on economic propaganda to sell cars or Proctor and Gamble spends to sell soap. In 1972, the USIA budget was $196 million; in 1969, the Soviet Communist propaganda budget was almost $2,000 million. In 1971, VOA broadcast 779 hours per week, compared with 1,889 hours by the Soviet Union and 1,324 hours by the People's Republic of China. Carl T. Rowan, former director of USIA, pointed out, "The Communists spend two dollars a year per free man to be subjugated whereas the total propaganda outlay of the free world is about two cents per man per year."

2. Americans distrust "propaganda" agencies. Congressmen question closely the USIA budget, the loyalty and patriotism of USIA employees has come under attack; and such noted and respected journalists as Walter Lippman have protested the use of propaganda by our government.

3. The USIA is under pressure to use the "truth" in its publications and broadcasts (although as noted, the selection of which truths should be told can be a propaganda device in itself.) The Soviet propagandists are under no such pressure and can use half-truths, distortions or out-and-out lies to influence the non-Communist world toward Communism.

4. In a free society like the United States, the flood of

foreign propaganda in and out of the country can be only partially curtailed by our government, while the Soviet Union and China can and do severely control information leaving their country and reaching their people from the United States.

But international propaganda has a non-governmental side, too, and the effects of this non-governmental propaganda cannot readily be controlled, as both the Soviet Union and the United States have sometimes discovered. For example, several years ago the Soviets agreed to a "cultural exchange" of motion pictures with the United States. In selecting the films, the Soviet representative seized upon the American film *Grapes of Wrath*. From the Communist point of view, the choice seemed ideal. The film was about poor downtrodden sharecroppers in the United States, and the film itself, based on a novel about the depression, was a protest against inhuman treatment by capitalists of these sharecroppers. This protest, however, was not the message picked up by the Soviet public. Instead, they wondered aloud at the fact that even an obviously poor family in the United States could afford a car—actually a broken-down truck—to travel in and could go freely for thousands of miles across the United States without official papers or hindrance.

Hollywood films, unfortunately, have also had a less desirable propaganda effect among foreign peoples. American movies over the years have made many foreigners believe the United States is populated by (1) people of great wealth, (2) gangsters, (3) wild savages. Indonesia's former President Sukarno, certainly no friend of the United States, once said he believed the messages of such American films helped bring about the Asian revolution against Westerners.

Critics of the USIA, aware that American advertisers have helped to build the economy by "selling" products, have wondered why the USIA can't sell democracy just as easily. to the world. The culture gap is not that easily bridged. What sells cars, television and dishwashers in the United States will not only *not* sell democracy abroad, but can cause resentment and bitterness. For example, the advertising slogan "For those who think young" worked well in selling a soft drink in the United States. In some parts of the world, however, Asia for example, glorification of youth is not considered admirable; in fact, it is considered ridiculous.

A recent advertisement for a cigarette in the United States advocated the cigarette for "the man who thinks for himself." The American virtue of individualism is not appreciated in a country like Cambodia where the common saying *kamake* means, "I am ashamed to be different." Americans honor hurrying, punctuality, efficiency. Not so in Latin America, where there is a belief that there is a lack of dignity in too much hurry.

The gaps stretch wide in many directions. The color white often means purity in the United States. White is the color of mourning in the Far East. Red—to which many Americans react as being dangerous, bloody, revolutionary—represents a happy holiday color in China.

The pitfalls of "selling" American-style democracy to the world are many. The deepest pitfall is the egotistical belief that the American "way of life" is the best way of life for every people and culture. (A country with the crime rate of the United States may not seem a particularly worthy society to a foreign country where people can walk at night in cities unafraid.) This is the same pitfall that also traps the Communists who believe Communism is the only way of life for every people and culture. (A Communist government that imprisons artists and writers who do not follow the government "line," as both the Soviet Union and China have done, may not seem a desirable society to other nations.)

Such pitfalls exist, but there is also solid ground. Although propaganda can color actions by governments, some actions speak louder than words. The Marshall Plan, by which the United States gave aid to many nations after World War II, and the United States missions to the moon were not intended primarily as propaganda. But they were, nevertheless, great propaganda successes for the United States.

The importance of presenting America's side of the story to the world, of influencing attitudes for, rather than against, the United States cannot be over-estimated. With the growth of instantaneous communications by satellites all over the world, there soon will be no people or home that cannot be reached and influenced by foreign propaganda.

One fact remains clear. Whenever our country stops trying to communicate, to influence others by the spread of favorable information; whenever we consider money spent on military hardware more important than money spent on winning men's understanding and friendship—then we have lost our standing as a nation more certainly and more finally than if we had been defeated in bloody battle.

Propaganda in the Future, OR Propaganda Prophecies

LET'S LOOK ahead. We are not just crystal gazing, because propaganda's role for the future is somewhat predictable from its role in our past and our present. Expanding in the present day, for example, are the following:

1. *Motivational research.*

Two hundred years ago, George Washington dressed some of his soldiers in buckskins and armed them with long rifles to make them appear to be the long-rifle frontiersmen feared by the British. He hoped his Fear-appeal propaganda would make British soldiers reluctant to fight and deter them from advancing too close to American positions. But General Washington could not be sure how much or how many British soldiers would be influenced by his propaganda effort. He was guessing.

Future generals will not have to guess. Neither will future advertisers, politicians, revolutionists and government officials. All those who practice propaganda on a big scale will first find out through motivational research just what appeals will motivate or "work" on their mass audience. The propaganda devices they use, based on virtually unchanging human nature and human reactions, need not change. But scientific guidance will help them decide what propaganda device will be most effective. This scientific guidance, called *motivational research,* is new and is developing in importance.

Let's see how it works today. Our favorite television program, "Colt '44," is taken off the air after only twelve weeks. We write a letter protesting, saying that we liked the program. The sponsor or the network replies that only 5 percent of the viewers agreed with us. Does that mean that all viewers were asked to state a preference?

No. The sponsor and the network relied on opinion polls, public polls much more scientifically planned than the early ones used in the McKinley-Bryan Presidential campaign. Today, psychologists and social scientists carefully select a few people by their social class, their income, their age, their interests and their geographic locations. In other words, they choose certain people as being representative of various "types" found in the total viewing public. From these few selected "types," the scientists determine what mass public reaction is toward any given program. Are they 100 percent right? Not yet, but the work is sufficiently advanced to have made opinion polls an accepted part of today's scene.

Who requests opinion polls today? United States government officials operating the Voice of America do, to try to find out how foreign audiences react to Voice of America broadcasts. Politicians and political parties do, to learn how the public is reacting to political campaigns. And more than anyone else, advertisers do. Since they are investing millions of dollars in their campaigns, advertisers do not want to rely on guesswork about what is going to appeal to their potential customers. In the future, programs like "Colt '44" will be subjected to motivational research even before they are filmed for television. Statistical polls will be used to determine whether the public is favoring situation comedy, violent adventure or science fiction for the coming year. Opinion polls will indicate the "right" appeals to use at the "right" time. Advertisements and commercials will be planned around these "right" propaganda appeals.

Motivational research in the future may not have to depend on polls conducted as they are today. Today, door-to-door questioning, telephone and recording devices are used. Improved electronic devices will in the future make it possible to make sweeping, virtually instantaneous polls to decide on the appeals to be used on any chosen audience. However, motivational research in the future may not depend too much on polls because a new science called *consumer psychology* may be used to measure public reactions on many things.

Already today, most advertising agencies employ social scientists to study whether a red box or a green box has more consumer appeal on a grocery shelf, or whether a tiger tail in a gas tank or a 1,000–1 chance to win a prize will pull more drivers into gas stations. This consumer psychology involves many methods at present and will involve many more in the future. For example, one such consumer psychology study, using cameras in grocery stores, indicated that the number of times a consumer blinked his eyes when he was looking at a product showed how much it appealed to him. Advertising agencies have been known to spend as much as three million dollars for a single such study. They know the study will be worth it. The results will determine their future propaganda choices of appeals and devices—with no guessing.

In the 1960's, Jim Jones watched a television broadcast of a national election campaign. Only 10 percent of the people had yet voted, and poll booths would be open in some parts of the country for many hours. But television broadcasters calmly showed computer figures of what the final results of the elections would be. Jim—and other viewers—were outraged. He said the broadcasts discouraged him from voting. He said they made his vote unimportant. He—and the others—protested. There was only one protest he could not make: that the computers were wrong.

We have said that, in the future, opinion polls and motivational research techniques will have sorted people into "types" so that it can be known in advance who and how many will be influenced by planned propaganda appeals. Computers can take this data and arrive at even more refined conclusions.

For example, let us imagine that we are members of the board of a big progressive corporation that sells its product, beer, all over the world. Beer can be used by any adult; beer can be made anywhere; beer can be offered at any price. We have to advertise to compete. We have to use many different appeals to reach many different peoples. We have to keep our advertising cost down or be forced to increase the price of our beer and lose customers.

We employ scientists who take the results of polls and motivational research data and refine these facts into mathematical formulas to feed into computers. We ask the computers to tell us how much to spend on advertising and the most effective combination of mass media to spread our advertising messages. The result is a highly efficient information program.

The cartoon is of the present day. Computers and scientific polling are progressing toward making voting almost unnecessary. On the next election you watch on television, see if "they" do not predict the results of the vote long before the complete vote is in. *Sidney Harris, copyright 1969,* Saturday Review

"You don't have to vote, Sam. The results were given three hours ago."

"Subliminal projection" works most effectively with moving pictures, such as television or film. Looking at the picture above, assume you are watching a television news broadcast about a United Nations vote. The newscaster says the small, "underdeveloped" nations have swung the vote against the United States. The picture of the United Nations buildings then appears on the broadcast. A picture of the Yangambi tribesman, complete with ivory beads and leopard's-teeth necklace appears also—but so quickly on and off that the viewer does not know he has seen the tribesman. How might this flash "subliminal projection" affect your opinion of who controls the United Nations?

The caption reads, "Ready—you tell it in Russian, 'Down with collectivism,' and I tell it in English, 'Get out of Vietnam.' That ought to set their space programs back a couple of years."

As one cartoonist sees the future, people on other planets may turn to use of "Confusion" propaganda strategy, playing off Americans and Russians against each other to delay the earthmen's advance into space. *Ed Fisher, copyright 1966,* Saturday Review

"Ready—you tell it, in Russian, 'Down with collectivism,' and I tell it, in English, 'Get out of Vietnam.' That ought to set their space programs back a couple of years."

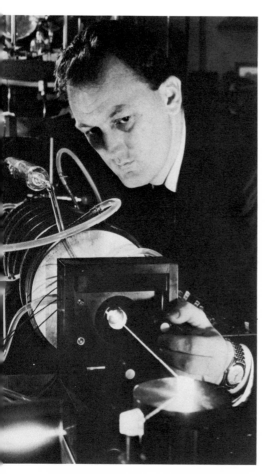

The Argon laser, emitting high-power blue-green beams continuously, can be applied to communications and spectroscopy. In the future, laser beams will allow three-dimensional images in films and television, transmission of many television channels over a single beam, information storage and retrieval, and many other functions too numerous to mention here. Assuredly, space communications is one future function, even from unmanned spacecraft 100 million million miles away. *Courtesy the Perkin-Elmer Corporation*

The Telstar II communications satellite, only 175 pounds and 34½ inches in diameter, receives, amplifies, and retransmits radio signals beamed at it from the ground. It is shown here as a model against an artificial background. But Telstar II has been used as a repeat for both color and black and white television, for one– and two-way telephone calls, for transmission of photo facsimiles and high-speed data, and for scientific data on its space environment. *Bell Telephone Laboratories*

Following his companion Neil Armstrong, Apollo 11 astronaut Edwin Aldrin takes the long step from the bottom rung of the ladder to the footpad of the lunar module *Eagle,* resting on the surface of the moon. Among the activities of the two first men on the moon were, significantly, the setting up of a laser reflector, a "telephone" talk with President Nixon, and television coverage of their work on the moon. The year was 1969. NASA administrator Dr. Paine predicted: "Man is indeed going to establish places of abode outside the earth. We have clearly entered a new era." *National Aeronautics and Space Administration*

The lunar module *Falcon,* of Apollo 15's mission, sits on the moon. To the bootprints of astronauts have been added the tracks of a Lunar Roving Vehicle carrying astronauts David Scott and James Irwin during their stay on the surface. Attached to the Lunar Roving Vehicle, which traveled 14.6 miles, was, of course, a television camera. The year—1971. *National Aeronautics and Space Administration*

This will be done a great deal, in the future, but it is already being done now. At least one progressive corporation, Anheuser-Busch, Inc., which sells beer around the world, tried this approach in the 1960's. Beer sales increased and advertising costs decreased.

Computers with their stored memories and speed calculation can be fed past and present information on the effectiveness of any of a number of Appeals in any given campaign with any given audience, and the computers will "mentally" digest this information and be able to tell what approaches should be chosen for new campaigns. Computers will be more effective than opinion polls and motivational research, because they will use both of these as aids in finding solutions to propaganda problems. Propaganda—the use of propaganda devices—can cease to be a hit-or-miss operation and become a highly calculated strategy with every passing year.

2. *Subliminal projection.*

At least one possible development in future propaganda will not depend on scientific automation. This development will depend primarily on our all too human reactions to what our senses tell us. Logic will have nothing to do with it. This approach to propaganda is often called subliminal projection.

Subliminal Projection, in its simplest form, resembles the propaganda devices of Loaded Words and Misleading Association. Thus, in the 1960's, "Winston tastes good like a cigarette should" was a popular and much imitated advertising slogan. Grammatically, the slogan should have read "Winston tastes good as a cigarette should." But the advertisers used the word "like" in order to imbed it in the consumer's mind subconsciously when he referred to or thought about smoking a cigarette. This Subliminal Projection of the word "like" was picked up by manufacturers of other products as well.

However, Subliminal Projection can be even more subtle. For example, as long ago as 1957, the words "Coca-Cola" and "popcorn" were flashed on a movie screen in a theater in New Jersey. The words were flashed on and off so rapidly that the audience was not conscious of having seen the words, superimposed as they were on top of a torrid love scene. Had the audience "seen" the words? None of them thought so. Yet the theater's sales of Coca-Cola and popcorn shot up remarkably that evening.

Later experiments showed that this same kind of subliminal approach, this subconscious appeal to the senses, could be used with sound tapes over radio, with listeners not aware they had heard any added words to affect their reactions to what they thought they had "heard" being said. Obviously, our eyes and ears see and hear more than our conscious mind realizes. Subliminal Projection is based on our human sensuous awareness—not our conscious logic.

How can this technique work in future propaganda? Well, let us picture a Presidential candidate giving a serious speech on our television screen in the future. Now, in the midst of his speech, picture a split-second subliminal view of a fool's cap perched on the head of the dignified candidate and split-second subliminal foolish words interposed with those he is actually saying.

Or let us picture a Communist delegate to the United Nations on television, speaking earnestly in favor of peace and disarmament. Then picture a knife "subliminally" placed in his hand. His speech is thereby discredited in the subconscious of the viewers. The subliminal picture or sound can, without our knowing it, influence our reactions and even distort what is actually being presented.

The subliminal approach, used as propaganda, sounds

potentially dangerous, and it is. For that reason, except experimentally, it has not been permitted on our national mass media today. But if this technique is already known and is not used, then why should it be regarded as an important possibility for the future? Because when one considers the future, questions must also be asked as to who will control mass communications and whether, on a world-wide basis, they can be controlled at all.

3. *Expansion of means of propaganda and communication.*

In the 1950's, the Iman of Yemen, chief of the small Middle Eastern country, was quoted as saying, "All one needs to make a government these days is a radio station and the declaration that you have made a government." Today, satellites can hover more than 20,000 miles above the earth and transmit television and radio programs, but the statement remains much the same, "All one needs to make a government is to control communications."

Radio, telephone, teleprint, teletype, newspapers, films and television are not new. Speed copying, automated libraries, satellite communications and laser-beam transmissions are all in varying stages of development. Scientists say that electronic pulses will soon be used to convert mass communication into any desired form in our homes. In the late 1960's, United Nations statisticians reported that two out of five people in the world could not read or write. One communicated with them by radio or in person. Many of them were not reached at all. But through communications media of the future all people will see and listen to something, and many of them to the same things. What they learn and what they do will depend on who controls what they see and hear. It is communication control, not propaganda, that offers danger for the future.

Propaganda is not just a "dirty" technique foisted on people. All people use it. Propaganda—the deliberate intent to persuade through chosen, usually emotional, material—has been a force throughout history because human beings have always wanted to persuade their fellows of something and have developed devices based on human reactions to accomplish this persuasion. Human nature is not going to change much in the 1980's or the 1990's or. . . . Communications will change, but not human nature or the propaganda devices based on human nature.

Most people think of propaganda as agitation for change. Two modern scholars of propaganda, however, Michael Choukas and Jacques Ellul, have pointed out that propaganda most often seeks to produce conformity, to gain popular support for things as they are, for the status quo. Conservatives as well as liberals use propaganda, and conservatives tend to be those propagandists with money and power who favor things as they are and seek to persuade the dissatisfied that they "never had it so good." Liberals have the opposite view and seek change. Continual presentation of both points of view make any radical change through propaganda unlikely. But if the balance between sources of propaganda alters, change of one sort or another can follow. As *The New York Times* said in an editorial as early as September 1, 1937, "What is truly vicious is not propaganda but the monopoly of it." Thus control of communication rather than control of propaganda must be the true concern of the future.

Certainly propaganda is not going to lose force and go away. Propaganda is an inseparable part of our lives. It both creates and satisfies our human demands. To disdain propaganda devices because men like Hitler used them is to disdain devices that men like George Washington—and ourselves—have also used. Our goals are different, but propaganda is a force used by all of us.

Because propaganda will become more and not less important if we wish to remain human beings of free choice, we must be able to discern the common devices of propaganda. If we know these devices, if we know the potentials of our mass media, and, above all, if we are aware of our own cultural and individual bias, we can find our way to what is nearly the truth—however much our emotions and senses are battered by conflicting views.

Nearly the truth? That is right: only nearly. Truth is not a certainty for us in all places at all times. We will have to make choices among shades of gray, because there is seldom really a choice between black and white, no matter how much propaganda would make it seem so. Our lives are searches for truth, and the end of our searching is the end of life.

In his poem "The People, Yes" Carl Sandburg refers to modern propaganda. His concluding stanza begins: *"The storm of propaganda blows always,"* but ends with these significant lines:

In the drive of faiths on the wind today the people know:
"We have come far and we are going farther yet. . . ."

Index

211